D1734460

BEHIND THE MASK

BEHIND THE MASK

TAMIE S. JOHNSON

ReadersMagnet, LLC

TABLE OF CONTENTS

PART I

I Had To Go Through It...11

Productive and Whole: Who I Was is not Who I am 14

Hope 19

Purpose in the Waiting 21

Times We Live In 25

In His Hands 28

Forever Grateful 30

The Struggle behind the Mask 32

Rising From the Ashes 36

Broken To Be Free 40

PART II

The NEXT 43

Building Under Construction 46

Behind the Mask 50

When Do We Grow Up? 53

I AM NEXT 55

How I Stand In These Shoes 57

My Choice for My Life...59

In the Room Again...63

Rebuilding the Wall/Family Relationship 65

Follow Me 68

Compassion and Encouragement 70

Healing for a Heart 74

PART III

He Called You Beautiful 77

Tailor-Made for This 80

Living It: Saved, Sassy, and Sixty 82

Looking for Myself 84

Ms. Sharon K Strength and Honor 86

Ring the Bell 89

F You #forgiveyou #forgiveme #forgivethem 92

Perspective and Anger 95

You Didn't Know 98

Letting Go while Holding On 102

Coming Home 104

Home for Thanksgiving 106

Moving Forward 109

I Am My Father's Son 111

My Mouth 113

Life's Lesson from Mama 115

Life's Rhythm 117

Being My Own Kind of Beautiful 119

A Better Me 121

Real Girls Rock 124

Hearing the Heart of Love Our Wedding Day 126

An Encounter with Love 129

Behind the Mask is something that many of us face in life if we are honest with ourselves. A mask can be social, emotional, cultural, traumatic, and relational. In my culture, it is said you better act like you got sense or whatever happens in this house stays in this house. When things go wrong and life happens, you are told to get yourself together and you pretend it didn't happen or just get over it. When it's traumatic, we hide and exhibit other signs, trying to hold it together when life happens. It's not just you or about you but it is facing yourself and being honest. I am in pain. I want and desire change in my life, but I can't do it on my own. We must learn how to deal with situations when life happens to and around us from our past and our now.

I want to say thank you to my family.

My mom sisters and brothers for their love support and encouragement; to continue writing what God gives to me. To my children LaShunda Terrance Tasha and Corrie Caden and our little Promise Baby Jersi Jade.

I HAD TO GO THROUGH IT

Wow! I did not think it would end like this; I didn't think it would be this hard. There were days I thought I was losing my mind and other times I just wanted it to stop. I wanted peace of mind, not this race replaying every scenario of the conversation over and over in my head. In this, I find myself looking for myself asking the real me. . . Will you please stand up?

There are times I want to quit but I can't because that is not who I am, and I was not built for quitting just because it gets hard. I stand tall and dig deeper, intensifying my praise. Praise is my weapon; prayer is the key. Faith unlocks the door, but I had to go through this, understanding that my this is not yours. All of us face challenges. Life happens. Just keep living.

Job said many such things are appointed to me but when he has tried me, I shall come forth as pure gold. I learned to praise and pray until it gets better. The old saints would say PUSH because it is no longer me. The Holy Ghost is working on the inside of me, walking me through the minefields. But I had to go through it.

This is a battle, and it is like being on the wheel and in the potter's hand. He said the clay was marred in his hand. Many times, people do not think they are flawed. We don't think we need to be reshaped or fixed. We blame others. But you have flaws too Boo, with our almost perfect self. Reshaping can be very intense and the hand that is doing the molding is not gentle. Many times, we tend to struggle against being shaped and molded. It is called not wanting to submit but you know somewhere in your knower it is working for your good.

Praying for change is one thing while waiting for the change to take place is a whole new thing altogether. When the change starts with you and in you, that is something else. I know I'm in His hands, but it does not look the way I think it should or want it to, but I had to go through this.

And he shall sit as a refiner and purifier of silver: and he shall purify the sons of Levi, and purge them as gold and silver, that they may offer unto the LORD an offering in righteousness. Malachi 3:3 KJV

For thou, O God, hast proved us: thou hast tried us, as silver is tried. Psalms 66:10

It is important to know God covers us in the mist of what we are going through. Often times we don't understand how he is working it out, but I know I want him to fix it…. fix them. But it is you, Boo, that he is working on. It's not about how you were treated or what someone said to you or about you. You messed up, too. Tell the truth. You said something also. Sometimes we need to hear what Paul said: "The good that I would do, I do not" and "the thing I do not want to do that I do." Just because it looks right to you does not mean it is right. You don't have to tell them off or get anyone straight. Check yourself. Just know He is working on you.

I am covered because of his love and grace; his mercy is new every morning. Great is his faithfulness. It is unmerited favor I can't earn. Do enough right to get it; I'm marred. He is LORD of my life. He protects me while he works in me. It is hard but I had to go through this.

³Oh that I knew where I might find him! *that* I might come *even* to his seat! ⁴I would order *my* cause before him, and fill my mouth with arguments. ⁵I would know the words *which*

he would answer me, and understand what he would say unto me. ⁶Will he plead against me with *his* great power? No; but he would put *strength* in me. Job 23:3-6

Job said, "Oh, that I knew where I might find him! That I might come even to his seat. I wanted to plead my case and explain what happened, but he already knows." Job said many such things are appointed to me, just know it is appointed to you also, the determining factor is how we will handle it. Sometimes we get full of ourselves, and pride comes in and we feel like we are doing the right thing, but you can be right and still be wrong. In this, I must ask myself what is the motivation behind it. It is important to be honest with yourself, **TELL YOURSELF the TRUTH.** What I sometimes miss in the lesson or test is I do not have to fight or prove anything. I must remain faithful and prayerful knowing that if He is not working on the situation, He is working on me in the situation. He covers me in the midst of what I am going through. He puts strength in me while the battle is against me, but it has already been won. But I had to go through it.

PRODUCTIVE AND WHOLE: WHO I WAS IS NOT WHO I AM

I thought it was over. I thought nothing was left. How can I go on living in this mess? I was sure I was finished — no hope of it getting better as I sit here looking back over my life, I ponder in my mind the things that transpired and brought me to this point. I recalled in that moment the stories I told myself. The mind is a complex battlefield. You can deceive yourself the way you perceive what has happened. You must be careful and ask yourself: can you be objective? And look at things based on facts and truth, or will it be subjective based on what is true in your mind. We must be honest and remember there is a cause and effect to every situation or circumstance.

There are situations that hurt us. What we go through and what is said to us play over and over in our mind, It becomes difficult for us to move on. The circumstance and cause are different for each of us. How it affects us or how we perceive it in our mind will determine how we get through it. The stories we tell ourselves — will it be supposition based on facts? or excuses?

There are things you may face as a child or young adult that carry over in life that cause you to feel less than you are. You hear your parent call you stupid and worthless, and that you are just like her/him, meaning who was talking and it wasn't a compliment. You know you have nothing to do with your birth or who your parents are, but that doesn't stop the accusation from being hurled at you like a missile hitting its target. It may be a different scenario. You meet someone who is so nice to you. He tells you that you are beautiful, and of course you believe it. Those words seem to be sincere. He told you he loved you: now he sees you desperate, and hopeful you believed him. Everyone wants to be loved, to feel accepted, and to know they're worth it. Now somewhere on this rollercoaster, things begin to change, and become a little confusing because love has now turned to control, manipulation, and abuse. And whether it's physical or verbal, abuse is abuse.

You are blamed for the acts committed against you as if you have control over another person's mouth or the emotional rage that fuels them. Now you are in shock. Were you tell yourself another story because you heard and saw small acts that you chose to ignore? Those were warning signs when little things are blown out of proportion. The difference is it wasn't directed at you, but it was there. The thing is when you want something you never had, you tell yourself a little piece of something is better than nothing at all, **Wrong.**

Now you're pregnant out of wedlock and even more alone than you were before and made to feel ashamed. The thing is no one told you that the baby isn't a mistake. Man can't give life; only God can do that. But you are told you're not worth it. Or *you're not much good to me now. Is it even mine?* Really. Now here's another trip shacking up, looking for love in all the wrong places. It doesn't matter whether it was the missed love and acceptance of a father or mother or the lack thereof from family, or a marriage that didn't last for one reason or another.

It's important to understand why you are BROKEN; the enemy wants to keep you in the dark about your identity. We find ourselves hurting and lost, not knowing who we are or the value and power we possess. We have gone through so much. We allow it to fester and cause us to be bitter, not knowing God wants to change us. We find ourselves in a place where we're not sure how we got there and unsure what to do while we are there.

There was a story I told myself in the midst of my misery, I told myself I deserved it because I wasn't good enough in my own eyes and I couldn't expect anyone else to see what I couldn't. I told myself I wasn't smart enough or I wasn't pretty or I was not enough because that's what I heard, and the treatment I received messed with my self-esteem. It's hard to hold your head up when you have no hope and you have forgotten how to dream. It's hard to be big when little things get you.

One day things changed because I had a conversation with Papa Daddy, my Heavenly Father. I talked to him about the impact of life circumstances and situations — the effect it had on me, and the lie we accept instead of the truth. He told me I was fearfully and wonderfully made and my soul knoweth right well. He called me his beloved and told me I was worth it, and His Son gave His life so that I could experience His love, mercy, grace, and his unmerited favor towards me. I didn't have to do anything to be good enough. His shed blood did that when I accepted him.

Oh, can you imagine how speechless I was that He would do this just for me. I wanted to know more, and I asked Him why He would do this for someone like me. He stretched out his arms and said, "so you can tell someone else what was done for you." Now I'm forgiven, healed, whole, and set free. He told me the story is what you went through but that's not who you are.... you are a child of the King. Your freedom was purchased by the shed blood of the lamb and the old man is dead and you are a new creation in him.

There may have been a thought in their mind that I wouldn't make it, or I wouldn't amount to much of anything. Because I was broken in my mind, I felt powerless to keep moving because I felt useless and thought there was nothing left. When I would have taken my life or just settled, someone was cheering me on, saying, "Follow me, chicken. Stay on the ground. But eagles soar. You can make it. I'll sustain you. You're not alone. You've been redeemed."

I was told a story about the olive and the process it goes through to become all it can be. What you see isn't all there is. There is so much more. The olive must go through a process to become productive. It is more than fruit on the tree in its natural state. The olive must be crushed and pressed. The process is not gentle. The mashing, pressing, squeezing, and crushing tears the flesh of the olive as it goes through this process. It is producing something that's pure. You see the former state of the olive wasn't the finished state. There was more it could give. What the olive goes through isn't the end, but a process that yields pure oil that make it even more valuable and productive.

⁸But I am like a green olive tree in the house of God: I trust in the mercy of God forever and ever. ⁹I will praise thee forever, because thou hast done it. I will wait on thy name; for it is good before thy saints. Psalms 52:8-9

I have learned that in my brokenness I have value and worth. I am productive. There are many levels to me becoming all he is calling me to be. I haven't arrived yet but I'm on my way. Don't count me out. There are things that will come about to try and keep me down, but it won't stop me. Knowledge and understanding are a powerful thing and when you discover the truth to know who he says you are, it does an awesome thing to motivate and encourage you.

To grant to those who mourn in Zion— to give them a beautiful headdress instead of ashes, the oil of gladness instead of mourning, the garment of praise instead of a faint spirit; that they may be called oaks of righteousness, the planting of the Lord, that he may be glorified. Isaiah 61:3ESV

Life is full of situations and circumstances and when you look back, you learn it didn't destroy you. Life happens to us all — the good the bad and the ugly. When you allow a loving Father to reach down and pick you up out of the mess and wash you in His love and show you who you really are, it makes all the difference in the world.

I'm made in His image. I'm made just like Him and the truth that is Him. He placed it within me. He gave me purpose for the brokenness because what didn't kill me just made me stronger. It helped me to be productive right where I am. There is something left. You may not feel it. Just know this: It's not about your feelings. It is on the inside of you.

We must understand that just because someone is broken doesn't mean he is not useful. He doesn't lose his value. There is still something left. He can use it and it will be a testimony later. Don't allow yourself to believe the lie or be fooled by the emotional rollercoaster. Even now if you are broken or in a semi broken state, I want you to know you are still productive. You are useful and you have value, and He will make you whole.

HOPE

I am waiting for the Lord, my soul is waiting for him, and my hope is in his word. Psalms 130:5 Bible in Basic English

Hope is a simple yet powerful word because to have hope fills one with yearning excitement like waiting for a special time in your life. You live with the anticipation that it comes to pass and trust that it will happen.

Expectation, desire, and trust — I do not see them, but I feel them with everything in me. Hope is not what you see with the natural eye, but you feel it deep within. You desire it, long for it, and you believe it will come to pass.

When the darkness falls, it seems all of your thoughts come pouring out. Even the wall and everything around you seem to speak to you when you are sorrowfully broken. The mind isn't silent, and your thoughts are everywhere, playing every scenario over and over. You have done everything you could think of except an interpretive dance. Your head is in a whirlwind of thinking and rethinking how it could have been different or better. What could you do to change it now? You feel as if you are hoping against hope. Thank God for Jesus for being a forgiving God, our redeemer. He restores even when we let him down. The scripture says that out of the depths. Another translation says, "I have great troubles. I am in a deep place, but my hope is in God and his redeeming power. My hope is that he will come to my rescue and bring the morning with peace and joy. Although the night is long and dark and there is no rest in this place that I am in, but my soul hopes in him. When there is no one to fall back on, I can fall back on him and meditate in his word, reminding myself what his promise is to me."

> ¹Out of the depths have I cried unto thee, O LORD. ²Lord, hear my voice: let thine ears be attentive to the voice of my supplications. ³If thou, LORD, shouldest mark iniquities, O Lord, who shall stand? ⁴But there is forgiveness with thee, that thou mayest be feared. ⁵I wait for the LORD, my soul doth wait, and in his word do I hope. ⁶My soul waiteth for the Lord more than they that watch for the morning: I say, more than they that watch for the morning. ⁷Let Israel hope in the LORD: for with the LORD *there is mercy, and with him is plenteous redemption.* ⁸And he shall redeem Israel from all his iniquities. Psalms 130 KJV

There is a lesson to be learned in hoping. It is something on the inside of you a desire or yearning that waits with expectation for that desire to come to pass. We are in a deep or dark place.

Unfortunately, our desire is for now and in the near or distant future. We people want what we want, and when it is not happening in our timing or when we think it is supposed to happen, we become impatient, and we set about trying to make it happen and call it a blessing.

We try or do everything including an interpretive dance, hoping things will work out the way we want it to. We think we are helping but we create a mess and then ask why it didn't work for us or why it is taking so long.

PURPOSE IN THE WAITING

I sit here thinking about life and this situation, and I know there's a story I tell myself. Why am I here? What is the purpose in all of this? I hear these words in my spirit. There is purpose in waiting. Twice I heard it very clearly, but I wanted to know what the purpose is. I sensed in my spirit. Don't allow your emotions to move you or distract you from purpose. There is purpose in waiting. I thought about David. He was anointed King at a young age. He was 25 when Samuel was sent to anoint him, and he was thirty when he was anointed the second time before setting on the throne. He reigned forty years as the King Israel.

I think about how he waited. Waiting wasn't easy; he was running for his life. I just want peace of mind and understanding. David went through something to get to his purpose. God had a plan. David had to wait for the plan of God to unfold. First Samuel talks about how Hannah had to wait. She was barren and desired a child, but she had to wait. There were tears and sadness being mocked, but she waited. I may not know his plan or what his purpose is for me, but I am confident in this: he knows me and he knows the end from the beginning. There are times I don't see how it will work out and there are many things I don't understand, but I know I will wait for God and not move ahead of him. There is a situation that I don't understand or know the purpose. I just want it to be over. But I have learned if I move out of the timing that has been set for me, I stand the chance of delaying or messing things up altogether.

There are times we want to know why it took so long., We would say in hindsight, "If I knew then what I know now, I would have done this." That's one of the problems with us. We always want to know and tell God how to do his business for us. We think it is our business. We come to him saying, "Lord, help me with this" in one breath And in the next, we want to give him instructions on how to handle this. If we knew how to do it, why didn't we just fix it in the beginning?

For us to wait is like detainment, foot-dragging, hesitation, delay, postponement, or a setback. Our understanding is limited. We don't pray asking God for understanding and to strengthen us in this place. It seems like a waste of time when we could be doing something more productive or interesting. The word of God tells us wisdom is important. It's the principal thing in our getting get understanding.

> *⁷Wisdom is the principal thing; therefore get wisdom: and with all thy getting get understanding. Proverbs 4:7*

> *The entrance of thy words giveth light; it giveth understanding unto the simple." "Order my steps in thy word: and let not any iniquity have dominion over me." Psalms 119:130,133 KJV*

Waiting is hard when it is happening to you and you want it to be over. I have learned it's better to get understanding and I realized that waiting is important. It is a place of preparation and expectation of what is to come. It is to tarry listen and watch. This may not be a place of comfort; my flesh just wants it to be over and done with. Sometimes we forget the lessons we are taught. It should be a reminder of what we have learned and heard.

When the struggle is not as intense, we can almost see our way. When we are being prepared to move into the next level, it's important that we realize God is preparing us for greater things. We can't allow impatience to set in and become annoyed and distracted from purpose even when we don't understand. It's important to remain focused and prayerful.

The word tells us that the entrance of his word gives light illumination and he gives understanding to the simple. The other verse asks him to order my steps that inequity will not dominate or have control over me.

⁴As arrows are in the hand of a mighty man; so are children of the youth. Psalms 127:4

Purpose is interesting. It is for us to discover with hope to learn and accomplish something. The intent of it requires your participation and involvement. It positions and its aim is to shoot you in the direction of God's plan that is laid out. Wow, God is so awesome. The word says, "Like arrows in the hand of a mighty man, so are the children of your youth." We understand that an arrow is positioned on the sight of a bow and the string is pulled back and the position arrow is sent forth. So are we.

²⁰My soul hath them still in remembrance, and is humbled in me. ²¹This I recall to my mind, therefore have I hope. ²²It is of the LORD's mercies that we are not consumed, because his compassions fail not. ²³They are new every morning: great is thy faithfulness.²⁴ The LORD is my portion, saith my soul; therefore, will I hope in him. ²⁵The LORD is good unto them that wait for him, to the soul that seeketh him. ²⁶It is good that a man should both hope and quietly wait for the salvation of the LORD "Lamentations 3:22-30

The struggle is not to destroy us. It is to strengthen us that we will run to the rock that is higher than we are. The word in Lamentation says, "My soul remembers and it humbles you when you recall that it was God's mercies that we were not consumed and his compassion doesn't fail but it is new every morning." Then it lets us know that our hope needs to be in God, and God is good and it is good for us to wait for him. When the word lets us know to wait, and while we wait, it brings us to purpose. But we don't look to ourselves. We look to God. Unfortunately, we often follow society — hurry up, get it done, hurry up and wait. Waiting teaches patients endurance and this brings understanding. Praise God for calling out to us and reminding us there is purpose in the wait. I can say with joy ,while the tears fall, "Lord, I don't mind waiting for there is purpose in the wait."

TIMES WE LIVE IN

We live in a time where people are less concerned about their neighbor or friends. Many do not consider or know their history. Young men and women walk around with feelings they cannot identify nor do they recognize where all of it started. Unfortunately, there are those who think this is just who they are. This is the way. I am never considering the root from which it came. What or who did you connect yourself to? There is little or no respect. There seems to be a sense of entitlement and maybe it's just a difference of opinion. Many don't ask for one reason or another then you have a generation growing up thinking the world owes them something.

In those days there was no king in Israel; everyone did what was right in his own eyes. <u>New King James Version</u> Judges 17:6

There is a scripture that says, "When there was no King in Israel, everyone did what was right in their own eyes." Have you ever wondered why you keep falling into the same trap without thinking that we should know better by now — same deal, just a different packaging? Without realizing that you keep doing the same things, you keep getting the same results. Some may think dysfunction is normal because I have done it this way most of my life. No, it's because we refuse to change our behaviors and change takes you from what is comfortable to the unfamiliar. There is a root cause to everything and the fruit of it is what has been allowed to grow.

Unfortunately, we do not always recognize the battle that rages against our mind — the way we face or handle problems that happen in our life. We hide our feelings, never questioning why, holding on to secrets because that was what we were taught to do. We never talk about what happens in our life or home because it's our business. What? Can it be the fear of someone knowing what's happening in our life knowing we don't have it all together as much as we think or perhaps we just want what happens here to stay here? We hope that when we go out, we can keep our mask in place hoping no one can see past what we allow them to see. We never allow anyone to know what is going on because of what we think they are thinking, or we feel they will just talk about us or judge us. When did that ever stop people from talking and making up stuff about other people without knowing the whole truth? Many of these behaviors have been passed on or learned by watching and hearing parents or adult conversations. Husbands or wives may say such foolishness as: "don't tell anyone what goes on in here," "it's our business," and "if it will make you ashamed, don't do it." What is it that we don't want anyone to know? Will it cause us to lose face in the family? Our children will look down on us because we have a problem that we won't admit even to ourselves.

Now a new generation is here, and they do things a little differently than we did as children. Where we just accepted what was told to us, they question everything, and want to test it to see if it will happen to them. But there is still a problem because what mama and daddy didn't deal with in their life, hoping it will die with them, is left for another generation to struggle with and they don't have a clue as to what's going on. Because no one talked about the elephant in the room, so to speak. This generation turns their backs on values that were taught as if they are beneath them, not understanding the struggles that others endured to afford them the opportunities they have.

We now find ourselves in a place of trying to understand what happened. We don't know because no one is talking about life and what you should know or what to expect. There is little to no preparation or knowledge when the past comes back to sit in your house. The way many find things out isn't because someone was talking to them. Some would try to eavesdrop, hearing bits and pieces of conversation the adults are having. Children eavesdrop because the adults' conversations are interesting and they don't want the children to know. Kids would sneak around, trying to hear bits and pieces of conversation, never getting the whole story or the truth.

Some of our parents couldn't read at all. Others didn't read well, but they had something that most of us don't have today and that's mother wit, knowledge you don't get from a book but is in you. There were things that got past them and there were those that tried to make a fool out of them or take advantage of them, but they understood the value of an honest day's work — to work hard, say what you mean, mean what you say, just be honest, and they wanted their children to learn.

I have learned over the years that when we talk about our feeling and learn how to deal with our pain, it helps us to heal. It's important for us to talk to our children to let them know what we went through and to know that it is God that brings us out of whatever we go through. Not telling the story isn't the shame. The shame comes in when we allow another generation to be ignorant of their past not knowing the struggle that will show up in their future. We have made mistakes but if we learn from the mistakes, we don't repeat them; we have grown from the knowledge to recognize what is going on.

A friend is a treasure who loves you as you are, sees who you are and who you can become, understands when you are at your worst and lifts you when you fall and loves you at your best, understand your past, believes in your future accept you as they share your everyday experiences encouraging you to be better and will come in when the world has gone.

IN HIS HANDS

Whose hands are you in?
This question came to mind
The weight of it I see is too great for me
Life in my hands is not all I want it to be.
So many times, I am just not sure,
how to handle the challenges I face
I look at my life and wonder what is going on.
In my hands, Life is fragile, fleeting, unsteady, it's a mess.
Feeling incapable of judging what's best,
Or who is, what's right in this
There are times I can't see the forests for the trees
blinded by the things I see and the things I don't see
my vision is obscured, unclear,
my thoughts are in disarray
life in my hands tend to be messy.
In His Hands it's clearer,
there is a new start
In His Hands, everything comes into perspective
I can believe Him when He says it is well
He knows the end from the beginning.
In His Hand, understanding the process.

He's the Giver of life, the Repairer of the breach.

In His Hand, life is restored

In my hands it is marred

In the hands of The Potter,

He made it again

In His Hands, it can live

In His Hand, it's yes and amen

every promise is yes and Amen.

In His hands there is a promise

A promise for you and me

I'm a new creation all things are new.

He won't leave me, He is with me to the end,

He bottles my tears and takes the pain away.

In my hands, its helplessness

In my hands there is indecision

In my hands I choose

I don't know how to get around this mountain.

In His Hand,

He said speak to the mountain and it is cast into the sea.

Everything about life can change in His Hands

He stretched them out, They were pierced for me

In His Hands, old things have passed away

behold all things are new.

In His Hand

I live nevertheless not I, but Christ lives in me.

Whose hand are you in?

I am in His Hands.

FOREVER GRATEFUL

There were times when I just didn't know how I would make it or if I could get through any of this. Life seems hard but as I look back, to see where You brought me from, I am forever grateful to You. Life will happen to us and around us if we keep living. It's not always the way you choose because mistakes sometimes make you feel as if you will never pick your head up again. There is that unseen foe that whispers to you and he brings your past back every chance he gets to keep you feeling bad about yourself.

I am so glad that I learned to listen to The Word and what You said about me. Because I can step in the spirit realm, to the unseen, of what you said in the beginning and bring it to my now, I am so grateful. You said that I am fearfully and wonderfully made even when I don't feel it. I have the mind of Christ and if I lack wisdom, I must ask of Him who gives to all men liberally lacking nothing. I have learned, not just for me but for my children, that it means I am academically astute. The capability that I have is not common. It comes from God. I am so grateful I saw myself as a failure. He didn't. When I thought me a loser, He didn't. When I thought I would never make it, He said I could, but I had to trust Him. When mean things were said to me and I was called everything but what mama named me, He called me His beloved, and He called me by my name. I am so grateful.

When I was told I was not worth it, He said, "You are because I died for you." I am grateful. When it felt like no one really loved me, and I told myself I was unlovable, He loved me. Even in my mess, shacking up looking for love in all the wrong people, kissing toads trying to find a prince, I am grateful. How does a single parent, trying to be a good example with a truckload of mistakes at every corner, do this and not scar them forever? How will they know that you love them? He said, "Point them to me and let them hear you say 'I love you' to each one individually and collectively." I am grateful because it's not about me. You gave me the right family for what I need, broken and dysfunctional, learning how to live not just exist, but to forgive and to love.

I am forever grateful to You. You didn't leave when the going was tough. You stayed right there and helped us through the storm, and You were with me even when I couldn't feel You. There were times I wanted to give up and quit but it was You who encouraged me to hold on. Although I didn't know it then, I am grateful. It took a while before I would give it all to You — children, husband, family, and every situation that's connected to me. Learning to say what You say about all of us, I am grateful because I am forgiven and I am accepted in the beloved. To know that I am loved so much that You would speak to the storms in my life, and speaking peace over us, I am forever grateful.

Learning how to live this life that seems out of sorts so that others may read it and know they have a chance, I am grateful. You loved me so much you wouldn't leave me where I was stuck and couldn't find my way out. LORD, I am forever grateful to You. To know you loved us so much that you continue to give us overwhelming victories through all these difficulties, I am forever grateful to You.

THE STRUGGLE BEHIND THE MASK

When the LORD asked Adam where he was, it was not that God didn't know where he was, but man had done something that brought change and fear to himself. Adam hid himself as if God didn't know he decided without considering the outcome. Man will hide the pain and struggle with excuses because he does not want to appear weak or less, never realizing that he has a choice. This is something he has never experienced before. This is the fall of mankind.

Choice is the right, the power and ability to choose — a decision made without force. Man chose to move in disobedience, and the word came to him first and now he hides and tells himself he is ok but he is not because he is afraid. It is easy to blame someone else, and not take responsibility for your actions. The man said it was the woman God gave him. It seems as if God and the woman were at fault because of the decision that he made. I can almost hear the explanation. *All this started because of the woman you gave me, all I had to do was name animals and insects and trees, but you gave me a woman.*

We may walk away from the responsibility of decision and there are times we may not count the cost and think it is okay even if we are wrong. It's called fear, insecurity, and doubt — sitting with your head in your hand, playing reruns about past failures and the uncertainty of life now, trying to put a finger on what went wrong, and the ifs of your life, holding on but needing to let go because you're unsure how it will play out, wondering if this is the right move or the right time. Pride comes in and you tell yourself you don't have to do anything — you are grown. It's like drinking poison but hoping for different results. This could have been different but what went wrong? You never admit that you were wrong and refuse to accept responsibility for your actions or what you said because you can be right and still be wrong. You never ask yourself what you can do to get back on the right track.

You worry about tomorrow, the future, and its cares, not realizing your right now is jacked up while trying to figure out what's ahead is not easy. You play the game in your mind: Does he/she love me? Is this like the last time? But never admitting you did wrong. Will this person accept me? But you are still holding on to things from the past and childhood hurts you refuse to let go even though you want to move on.

You have self-doubt and the struggle of being enough: Does anyone really love me? Or am I just fooling myself? You can't see value in yourself so you can't see value in anyone else. You tell yourself this is my life and I do what I want to because I am a man. You tell yourself: I did my best but no one appreciates me. Your inability to ask for help and your struggles hold you captive in a will that is not yours. It belongs to someone else.

There is a strong hold in your life and if anyone tells you that you were wrong, you find a way to cut them off. You tell yourself that you are okay, and everyone is against you. You do not have a problem but there is a rage on the inside that rears its ugly head more often than you like.

You wear a mask to keep others at a safe distance while telling yourself you're okay. You stand alone in a room filled with people but do not engage with others around you. You are aloof in the midst of people, hoping no one can see the real you. There is a problem, and you live in fear of someone finding out that it is not what it looks like, never understanding or realizing that we are fallen — broken people in need of a healer.

You think safety is hiding behind a mask but anyone who studies people will see there are cracks in that façade — pain and disappointment — and someone is hiding. There have been some painful circumstances, disappointments, and rejections in life for you and feeling let down is hard and you just cannot seem to shake it. But before you let anyone hurt you, you will hurt them first or run. People who are hurt always hurt other people.

Jealousy, manipulation, verbal abuse, and blaming others – these occur because of what is lacking in you. You find a reason to get angry about nothing and before you answer a question, you will start an argument. Never wanting to answer the question about what is going on, you start another quarrel — same argument, just a different tactic, saying things that have nothing to do with the issue at hand. Name-calling and derogatory verbiage only speak about your character.

From an adult perspective, why not talk and look at it from a different view? Since you are man, head of the house, why are you complaining? But I already know your attitude — let me get you before you get me! But that is not my mindset because I do not want to hurt you.

Living behind a mask, trying to appear normal, or hiding your feelings is such a chore. It comes out anyway because it's the little foxes that spoil the vine — hiding the fear of rejection, unsure of who loves you, and wondering if you can trust or believe that everyone is not out to get you. You live behind the mask because you do not want to face the truth, or you do not know how.

You want someone else to blame for your life — how someone hurt you. But you hurt someone, too. You are unsure of your value and unsure of your self-worth, and no matter how many times you are encouraged, you doubt that it is for real and you must not be talking to them. The struggle is real and the pain you feel is real. There is no shame because I can say I was there, too, but Someone came into my life and called me out of hiding. He will do it for you also. Now leave the mask and ask Him to come into your life for real.

> [34]Therefore do not worry about tomorrow, for tomorrow will worry about itself. Each day has enough trouble of its own. Matthew 6:34

RISING FROM THE ASHES

"To appoint unto them that mourn in Zion, to give unto them beauty for ashes, the oil of joy for mourning, the garment of praise for the spirit of heaviness; that they might be called trees of righteousness, the planting of the LORD, that he might be glorified." Isaiah 61:3 KJV

Days turn into weeks, and weeks into months, and it seems as if I'm stuck in a place of despair. All I see are ashes and despair. I want to move forward. When thinking of something I need or can use, I'm reminded it has been turned into ashes. How do I arise from this place of mourning and sorrow? How do I get up and start again? I didn't think it would hurt so much or last this long. It is so out of my element of control. Now what do I do? Will the real me please get up!

This is a place that is unfamiliar. Although I have gone through hard times before, I wonder what made this so hard. Life is not always what we hope. It is often hard and sometimes unhappiness comes to shake things up a bit — unhappiness because of pain felt in loss, betrayal, abuse, judgments, abandonment, divorce, and death, depending on where your mind is. It could change the trajectory of your life.

This reminds me of Job and what it must have been like for him when friends accused him and his wife told him to curse God and die. Wow! How do you withstand such misguided advice that affects not only you, but them, too? Daniel, in captivity, taken and accused by jealous, envious people who didn't understand who he was and the call on his life. But he is thrown into a lion's den because of someone else's deceitfulness.

Tamar was desired by her brother and instead of treating her with respect and dignity, she was raped and tossed aside as if she was wrong and looked at as if she was disgusting. But he was the one who did that to her. Dinah, the daughter of Leah, was raped in the field because someone desired and wanted her. She lived in shame. Joseph was sold into slavery by his brothers and taken away from his home and father. These are ashes and in the mist of it all, a sovereign God was there. It didn't catch Him by the surprise it throws us. We can't get our footing. We feel lost in a tailspin, but He is not. There is purpose in the things we suffer from but we are the ones who don't understand or know why.

He said he would give us beauty for ashes, and the oil of joy for mourning, the garment of praise for the spirit of heaviness. I ask the question: Will I ever regain my footing and will we ever be okay again? Whatever it is, I hope that the tide will change, and the sun will shine in this place of despair and darkness. I want to be strong and stand tall knowing it is working for my good and I know it's not about a feeling because emotions change. Feeling can be deceptive and fleeting because you think one thing, but you never ask where this is coming from or if it is subjective or objective.

In this I must tell myself the truth. This did not catch God by surprise and to lose one thing He may be preparing me for more. Just because I can't see it doesn't mean He is not working in the midst of what I am going through. The enemy uses this opportunity to make God look bad to me, but I must come to myself and let him know I see him and God is still faithful. He is with me when I can't see His Hand. He is with me when I cry myself to sleep. He is with me in the ups and downs of life, and he has never left me alone.

This is a temporary place that I am in right now, but I know I am not alone. There is nowhere that I go that He is not there. There is nothing that happens that is unknown to God. He is ever present. Nothing is hidden from Him. David knew this when he wrote Psalm 139.

> ¹O LORD, You have searched me and known me. ²You know when I sit and when I rise; You understand my thoughts from afar. ³You search out my path and my lying down; You are aware of all my ways. ⁴Even before a word is on my tongue, You know all about it, O LORD. ⁵You hem me in behind and before; You have laid Your hand upon me. ⁶Such knowledge is too wonderful for me, too lofty for me to attain. ⁷Where can I go to escape Your Spirit? Where can I flee from Your presence? ⁸If I ascend to the heavens, You are there; if I make my bed in Sheol, You are there. ⁹If I rise on the wings of the dawn, if I settle by the farthest sea, ¹⁰even there Your hand will guide me; Your right hand will hold me fast. ¹¹If I say, "Surely the darkness will hide me, and the light become night around me"— ¹²even the darkness is not dark to You, but the night shines like the day, for darkness is as light to You. Scripture Psalms 139:1-12 in a Psalm of David

When I read this, I know that he will give us beauty for ashes. I can't see it because my feelings and emotions are deceptive, but the truth is, God is faithful. He will not leave me in the place of sorrow. It is a choice that I must make. I can sit in a place of sorrow and dwell on the ashes and what is lost or I can rise and receive the oil of joy for mourning because mourning doesn't have to be a bowed head hanging low and red rimmed eyes. It can be the joy of the LORD strengthening you in the midst of it all.

Life will happen but I choose to learn something here because Jesus paid for it all. Sin left a stain but the blood of Jesus washed me. The song says,

"What can wash away my sins?

Nothing but the blood of Jesus.

What can make me whole again?

Nothing but the blood of Jesus."

I have a choice. I will rise from the ashes, and put on my garment of praise. The word lets us know. In everything, give thanks for this is the will of God, in Christ Jesus, concerning you. Get up from the ashes and sing praise, allowing the spirit of joy to fill your heart.

BROKEN TO BE FREE

His divine power has given us everything we need for life and godliness through the knowledge of Him who called us by His own glory and excellence. *2 Peter 1:3*

I was wounded in the house that I grew up in — just a boy child, not yet a man, working to make a living. Rejection and disappointment made me unsure of the world I was living in. The thought in our mind causes us to make decisions based on our reasoning and circumstance. I walked away from the place we lived as a field hand, young and not sure of my destiny, but I wanted a place. I wanted a home.

My only clothes were in a paper bag and what I had on my back. I knew there had to be something better than this and somewhere there is a place in this world for me. I was traveling along a lonely highway, hot and dusty rocks getting in my shoes, in search of a place for me to call home.

You don't know my story or how this came to be, but I put what I left behind in a place for no one but me. In my mind I can forget and never speak of it again — a secret — a time and place I just want to forget.

For whenever our heart condemns us, God is greater than our heart, and he knows everything. 1 John 3:20

It's not what I thought, and it didn't turn out as I planned it in my mind. I was in control of life, or so I thought. We make decisions and choices based on past experiences, feelings, and emotions. We view life through the lens of pain, disappointment, and rejection and often wonder if the sun will ever shine for us again.

We all have a story and we don't always understand the mindset and why people do the things they do. Sometimes we judge others harshly, but we don't know their story or pain. I just want you to do better without ever understanding what brought you to this place. It's the choices and decisions that we make that are life-changing and long-lasting.

This reminds me of Job. The scripture says he was just an upright man who feared God and abstained from evil. But in reading this scripture, I find his friends judgmental they made accusations concerning what has happened. Feeling rejected, he sat in the ashes of life with broken people assuming.

The story of the olive is remarkably interesting. It must go through something to get the best out of itself — to realize its value. It is picked and debris is removed. Then it is cleaned and washed. You may think that's not so bad, but that's not all there is to it. The process will be hard because pressing, crushing, and having the flesh torn to get to what you are called to be isn't easy. The olive has a pure oil that is released from it.

So it is with us as it was with Daddy. He had a story and he had to go through something to reach his destination. Many times, we forget to include God in our journey through life. Sometimes we leave him out and when things go wrong, we wonder why he didn't rescue us from this awful time in life. But the great thing is God is with us in our journey through life. He is waiting for us to acknowledge and ask Him to direct our life.

I believe Daddy had a relationship with Him. It is so important, and he settled some things and got it right on this side. Maybe it wasn't the way we wanted it to be but it wasn't our call. It was his. He talked to God and God talked to him. As it was with him, so it must be with us. We all have a destination. Make sure you include God in your life. Make sure your election and calling are sure.

> **Nevertheless, the foundation of God standeth sure, having this seal, The Lord knoweth them that are his. And, Let everyone that nameth the name of Christ depart from iniquity. 2 Timothy 2:19 New King James Version**

Therefore, brethren, be even more diligent to make your call and election sure, for if you do these things you will never stumble;

THE NEXT

I will stand upon my watch, and set me upon the tower, and will watch to see what he will say unto me, and what I shall answer when I am reproved. Habakkuk 2:1

I will hear what God the LORD will speak: for he will speak peace unto his people, and to his saints: but let them not turn again to folly. Psalms 85:8

What is The Next and who can go there? Is it a place, a time? Is it a movement — a call to duty to transcend from normal to greater? Understanding how to get there or move in it is important for us. It is a way of life for believers. It is seasons of change, and God calls us to change. A season, a mindset, an attitude must be conformed to God's will for our life and our desire is to be all He has called us to be. The Next isn't just a word or phrase or a good conference name. It is a transcending word, following, succeeding to surpass, upcoming, going above and excel beyond what you think you've done, but in adjacent to His Will.

The Next is moving priceless women into position and we must be ready. It is important to be prepared, ready to move and listen for the instruction that will be given. We move forward and you have to rise in expectation of the Next. I heard preparation is everything. You don't want to go into battle unprepared or start a journey and not know where you are going. We have to redevelop or condition our lives in a new normal but keep moving and continue to rise above the norm. What many don't realize is we are being prepared and conditioned.

The scripture says, "I will stand upon my watch. Set me upon the tower. I will watch to see what He will say unto me, to listen and hear to get understanding."

He said, "Rise! Get up from the place of complacency. Don't just desire change but be the change."

He is like a refiner fire and the purifier of silver, and we said, "I want to be tried by fire, purified, LORD, we need a refreshing move. We don't know when it will happen, but the desire is being borne in us.

Preparation and understanding are everything. I heard a message "Moving to my Next" when the children of Israel got ready to move. They made preparation. There was blood on the door post and death passed over that house. While prayer and praise took place, they received instructions and they spoiled the Egyptians. They left Egypt loaded. The Next requires preparation and there is no time for a lot of questions. When the Spirit of God prompts you, listen to hear and do what the Spirit is saying. He said in this season LOVE DOES and He is ALIVE.

We need to know what love does and who love is. We are to be reminded daily that He got up and because He is alive, we can live. The Next is knowing we have to rise from dead places and complacency, to understand our differences and still be Christ like. We have to move forward to rise in unity — one voice, one sound.

There is a call for love and learning — to love for real. It is not what we say but what we do and to know the father's heart. "Love shouldn't be a word that comes and goes, this should be our daily walk and it gets better as we grow."

Being tried by fire is not just a passing fad. It is a lifetime of being purified because we are being changed and renewed every day. We have said or done things that did not bring glory to God. Please don't act like you got it all together. In the Next, we must speak truth to life, and it will take us deeper and higher. We can no longer stand and be content with a superficial walk, unprepared, waiting for someone else.

Our desire is for the LORD to see his image in us, and we want to thoroughly surrender to the Father's will. The women of this house are perfectly-shapely shades of power and strength, same but different, Dunamis power, called to speak the truth. But like Him, to be the change, we want others to see as the body of Christ.

Hear the clarion call to The Next.

BUILDING UNDER CONSTRUCTION

According to the grace of God which is given unto me, as a wise master builder, I have laid the foundation, and another buildeth thereon. But let every man take heed how he buildeth thereupon. 1 Corinthians 3:10 King James Version

Life and our spiritual walk are and can be like a house or structure. You are a building and before you can proceed with the building process you must do several things. You may need a blueprint and to purchase property; you may need to get a permit to build the structure in a particular location. You will need to know the design and how large or tall this structure will be before proceeding.

I praise God that I have already been purchased. I was bought with a price and the shed blood of Jesus paid it all and His resurrection is my permit. I don't have to buy what has been given to me already. But I do have to make sure that I am current in the deeds and to know if it lines up with the Word. If it a new structure I must do a soil check.

I may have to remove the old soil that's my old mind set and thought process, and bring in new soil called renewing of my mind before I can lay the foundation. It's important that I get a billboard revelation about my life, stating to myself: Coming Soon. I must also determine what I want in this building that I am building, and how I want the structure to stand.

Now being under construction can also mean renovation of an existing structure, meaning you have been in the way so long. You may have to gut it out, and put in a new wiring and enlarge areas, or make them smaller, more compact, depending on what you need. We must know what is coming into our life. We can't afford to build on just anything, and we can't afford to allow just anybody to build on our foundation, meaning you must be careful who you allow to pour into your life. The scripture says:

> **⁴For every house is builded by some man; but he that built all things is God. Hebrews 3:4KJV**

Therefore, we must know who is doing the building and who is laying the foundation of this building. As we look around this world we live in, sometimes you can't tell the church from the world. Everybody wants to know of the LORD, but no one has time for Him, meaning: Do you have a relationship? Or are you like Israel? They knew His deeds and what He provided for them, but they didn't have a relationship with Him. The scripture says God knew Moses face to face. He made known his ways unto Moses.

He was seeking his hand but he had no time to be acquainted, to have a relationship with him, to be taught his heart. I want the goods but I have no time to allow the Word to get in me and build and change me in my prayer life. We don't make time to do general maintenance on our life structure. In a house you must do repairs because faucets leak, pipes freeze, gutters need to be free of debris, and doors and windows stick or become loose and need adjustments, and some things just wear out if you're not careful. We can start to fall apart by letting the little things go and not allowing time for repair.

> **³⁷For yet a little while, and he that shall come will come, and will not tarry. ³⁸Now the just shall live by faith: but if any man draw back, my soul shall have no pleasure in him. Hebrews 10:37-38**

Every day of our life we are under construction. We need to work on something. It may be our attitude, prayer life, our faith walk, our love walk, and learning to trust him in every area of our life. It's learning to extend grace and mercy to others not because of them, but because of Him. He extends mercy to us every day. Sometimes it's our attitude of entitlement, the feeling that we deserve this. The question is how grateful are we in this season of our life? You see, it's the little foxes that spoil the vines, the little things we allow to creep in with the potential to disrupt life as we know it.

Songs of Solomon 2:15 will let you know how well you handle the struggles and trails you face; are you angry, bitter, complaining or do you play the blame card? When we do self-check, we don't have time to check anyone else. We are trying to get and keep our building straight and up to code.

> [32]**But call to remembrance the former days, in which, after you were illuminated, you endured a great fight with afflictions;** [33]**Partly, while you were made a public display both by reproaches and afflictions; and partly, while you became companions of them that were so used.** [34]**For you had compassion on me in my bonds, and took joyfully the spoiling of your goods, knowing in yourselves that you have in heaven a better and an enduring possession.** [35]**Cast not away therefore your confidence, which has great recompense of reward.** [36]**For you have need of patience, that, after you have done the will of God, you might receive the promise. Hebrews 10:32-36 KJ 2000**

In the construction business you will deal with delays for one reason or another. So it is in life. How will you handle these roadblocks? Have you considered fasting prayer and reading and studying the word to help in that area? Have you asked yourself what the scripture has to say about it?

[3]And I sent messengers unto them, saying, I *am* doing a great work, so that I cannot come down: why should the work cease, whilst I leave it, and come down to you? [6]So built we the wall; and all the wall was joined together unto the half thereof: for the people had a mind to work. Nehemiah 4:3,6

There will be days that you are marking time, as the old folks say, but don't get discouraged or weary in well doing because it will surely come. This lets you know that it is necessary to be watchful, prayerful, and ready because life happens, ready or not, and it doesn't care about your plans. You must always be ready, making sure that your structure stands and is free of anything that will cause it to fall or land in decaying state.

[1]I will stand upon my watch, and set me upon the tower, and will watch to see what he will say unto me, and what I shall answer when I am reproved. [2]And the Lord answered me, and said, Write the vision, and make it plain upon tables, that he may run that readeth it. [3]For the vision is yet for an appointed time, but at the end it shall speak, and not lie: though it tarry, wait for it; because it will surely come, it will not tarry. Habakkuk 2:1-3

BEHIND THE MASK

Behind the Mask is fear, low self-esteem, doubt, attitudes of brokenness, pain and the uncertainties of life. There's a story I tell myself because of what was spoken to me or about me in anger or caused me to feel bad. The queen crown doesn't sit as it should because it's bent and leans to one side unevenly, you might say. Trying not to show this part of me to everyone, I hide behind a mask, afraid of being rejected. You see the part that I feel safe showing. It's the part that looks put together and has hardened through the course of time. You see the smile and hear the laughter; you see the air of confidence that is not real. I walk with my head up and shoulders back with the attitude that "I have it together" or the look that says, "I have arrived, but I know it's not true."

There is a part of me that's hidden away that only He knows and sees — untapped potential, shame, guilt, brokenness, rejection, and abandonment — trapped as if it's in stone. It is the shame of what happened and the fear of someone finding out — that I am not as together as I appear to be. The queen-me hides because I'm not all I want or desire to be. Generational strongholds in my life and the harsh words spoken in anger that keep repeating themselves in my head won't allow me to be free. The lies I was told, the shame of a lifestyle that's out-of-control, feelings of defeat and misunderstanding — I don't want to repeat.

I live like I got it going on, like I have an oil well in my backyard, standing at the Mac counter, wearing red bottom shoes and carrying a

Brahmin bag, but you can't follow me home. This is the me you see. This is the me that want to stop fronting and just be real. I want to be free to be me. Behind this mask, I feel that I'm a prisoner in stone.

Oh, it not the type of stone that you can see but it's there weighing heavily on me. I dress it up and make it look good but it's like the irritation that an oyster feels from a grain of sand that gets into its shell. When the oyster feels that irritant, it releases or secretes something called nacre to cover it. This builds up over time and produces a pearl. That irritation that an oyster feels may become a valuable pearl, but yours is keeping you bound.

Lips that spoke of love, honor, and respect now hurl words spoken to hurt. The power of words spoken in anger are hurled at you like a missile hitting its target. They are words spoken to break you down, and they last longer than you want them to. They play over and over like a bad record on repeat in your mind. You are okay in the crowd and at church, faking it till you make it. You can't see it's holding you down and keeping you from purpose to become all He is calling you to be. You Never allow anyone to get too close, forever striving, but never really achieving the victories you want. The word tells us to cast down thoughts and imaginations and every high thing that will exalts itself against the knowledge of God and bring those thoughts into captivity to the Obedience of Christ.

> **5Casting down imaginations, and every high thing that exalteth itself against the knowledge of God and bringing into captivity every thought to the obedience of Christ; 6"And having in a readiness to revenge all disobedience, when your obedience is fulfilled. 2 Corinthians 10:5-6**

You are home alone and the mask is removed — alone with your thoughts and no one can see you but you. Emotions don't come with manuals, but you can learn from the hurt and the pain that's been inflicted. You can get angry, but you don't have to sin in the anger. You can cry. It's okay. Validate your feelings. They are real, but you don't have to wallow in the pain of rejection, disappointment, or any of the other stuff that comes with it.

We must forgive ourselves and forgive the one that caused the pain, and we must let go of the hurt and stuff from our past. Stop reliving it. Instead of listening to the negative stuff bouncing off the walls, get a praise in your mouth. Oooh it's hard. It can be but do it anyway and it's okay if you cry. You don't have to pretend that you are oblivious to pain. The enemy wants to keep you silent and bound. Surround yourself with people who encourage and build you up. Get yourself an "I-am statement" — something you can hold on to and believe for yourself.

"My mask is gone, the Master set me free." The stone that held me has been chiseled away. The thing that kept me hidden is no longer with me, and all the other names are fading away. He will complete the work in me and now I know who I am.

I learned that I am who God says I am. His words say I'm fearfully and wonderfully made, and my soul knows right well. I am the head and not the tail. His word says to me that no weapon formed against me shall prosper. He says in the Word He would not leave me nor forsake me. His Word says I can decree a thing and it shall be established. I understand that weapons will form but they will not work in my life. I am learning to recognize the lie, and tell myself the truth. I have learned to surrender it all to God because it's in Him that I win, and He who loves me and gives me overwhelming victories in all these difficulties.

WHEN DO WE GROW UP?

When do we truly grow up and stop being wounded children, playing the victim all the time? We can't see the future for we are looking at our past. At some point, we should say in our minds that it stops here. You can no longer make a victim out of me.

We all have a story to tell. In the words of mama, we all have a cross that we must bear. She said Jesus had a cross that he bore for me and you and he carried it all the way to Calvary. He stumbled as he went because of what was coming behind him — a falling generation.

Now what makes you think you are any different? He paid for things He didn't do; He didn't lay the blame on them or you. He said, "Father, forgive them, not my will but your will be done." Why is it so hard to admit you were wrong?

Now here you are walking around here with your head in your hand and don't want to speak, laying the blame on anyone else. It's them, not me, everywhere except at your feet. It's not me, it's you, and it's your fault we are here. What! Walking around with this woe-is-me, didn't you know that you would have a lot that would fall to you?

Get over yourself and square your back with this sad woe-is-me. I am good. I am right. Why am I treated this way? Life happens to all of us. It's not always good and sorry to say, it's not always fair. So stop walking around here acting like it only happens to you with your head down, feeling sorrow for yourself.

We all have a cross that we must bear and yes, it can be hard but you're not alone — only if you want to be you. See, you have a Helper and you can call on Him anytime you need.

My grandma used to say, "Baby, you have a Helper, you know. You can call on Him when you can't see or know your way. When life overwhelms you and you're stuck in a rut, He'll bring you out and that's no lie. Don't let that devil keep on deceiving you with his cunning ways and lies. You can fight back. Don't be his victim. Use the Word. He has to flee."

When do we truly grow up and stop being children, playing the victim all time? We are childish in our actions, blaming, feeling pity, feeling sorry for ourselves as if no one else has a hard time. Oh, please me give me a dime for your time.

God won't come to a pity party. I hope you know, but he will come to a praise party. You must learn how to cast all your cares on Him. He's the only one who can see inside your storm and speak peace. Allow him to lead you as you praise your way out.

I AM NEXT

I am the woman
who faced the mirror and said out loud
I am Next.
Next to rise above disappointments and pain
Realizing that brokenness and the mess that I just stepped over
won't stop the plan of God
and delayed isn't denied.
I am Next
I am the woman
who turned the stones thrown at her into steps
because I refuse to give up
I speak life to situations and circumstances
I speak to where I am going not where I am
I am the woman
who speaks to purpose
commanding it to come forth.
The word says I can decree a thing
and it shall be established
I am Next
I decree that blessing and favor follow me
I am the woman who looks at my sister
And tell her, fix your face, Boo
don't give up
you're next
Dream big and reach up
Reach out, pull another sister up

Because I refuse to go without you
We are Next
I'm the woman
Who's willing to shatter
glass ceilings of stereotype and complacency
That's in place to hold us back
I am Next
A woman who knows who I am and Whose I am
I am the woman that has fallen and got back up
I know shame won't kill me
And I'm not afraid to say, 'me too."
I am the woman who
stands on the shoulders of prayer warriors
And intercessors
Standing in the gap, to make up the hedge
and reminds herself she's
tailor-made for this.

I am Next

HOW I STAND IN THESE SHOES

[10]*And the God of all grace, who called you to his eternal glory in Christ, after you have suffered a little while, will himself restore you and make you strong, firm and steadfast.* 1 Peter 5:10

I heard someone say I wish I were in her shoes. She got it so easy. Speculation — I thought, smiling to myself. She doesn't know. I wonder sometimes how I stand in these shoes. Thinking back before I got to this place in time looking at myself in the mirror, knowing it was a journey and it wasn't by chance. There was a price to be paid and lots of tears while holding on to a dream. Things don't always work out as we plan, but we hope.

Honestly, you don't know what you are asking for and you don't know the cost of what you will endure to stand in these shoes. You don't know my story and I don't know yours, but I know you don't just arrive without bruises or tears and there are no genies in a bottle to grant your wish. There is a cost, and you must learn a few things on this journey called life and it's not cheap. You feel that you know who you are, but you don't have those experiences to draw from. You haven't been anywhere or done anything. You don't know what you can take or how much you are willing to put up with or what you will lose.

Time, tears, pain, rejection, disappointment, and uncertainties — you can't see what it is or how to reach it. All you know is you want it and this is called training shoes in life for the call. I am sure you wonder why I call it that, but life has a way of teaching and training us through our experiences. Some of us get it. There are quick learners. For others, it takes time trying to understand what you are called to do. I can tell you to stand in these shoes. You face things you never dreamed you would. I was naive, sheltered, and protected although I had children. I kept them close just like my mom did me and my siblings. This scripture lets me know that there will be suffering but there will be restoration. Growth will take place.

Many times, we don't realize trouble has many faces. You must be able to discern what is what. To trust God and take him at His Word is one thing but unfortunately life happens. Just keep living. There are motives for actions, and you must stay prayerful so you can discern. I don't have time to fight about things that don't make sense to me and cause me to lose my focus. I don't have time to pine away the time wondering if I could've or should've because all I have is right now.

I stand in these shoes because of grace and mercy, not because of my goodness or how smart I think I am. It is because of God's mercies that we are not consumed, and they are new every morning. I stand in these shoes because I know life is full of decisions and choices we will make and if you are not careful, you can miss the moment.

It takes too much time going over the past and not enough for what is before us now. I stand in these shoes because I choose to love through the difficulties. We have painful circumstances sometimes and even in the time of pain I still must be honest with myself. I want to feel small when I stand by the ocean watching the waves come in. It is amazing to watch how the sky and water seem to meet but there is a dividing line that we can't see. I want to learn how to love through the discomfort of difficulties because I know I serve a big God who is teaching me in this training of life how to trust him as I stand in these shoes.

MY CHOICE FOR MY LIFE

²³Jesus said to him, If you can believe, all things are possible to him who believes. ²⁴Immediately the father of the child cried out and said with tears, Lord, I believe; help my unbelief! Mark 9:23-24

We live, love, and laugh, and sometimes we lose in life through the good, the bad, and all the in between, such as ups and down, highs and lows, that life brings. I am so glad that I have a choice and I can choose what I want and how I want to feel or what I want to do and how I want to live. I choose to love you through the difficulties and the pain but still be honest with myself. I choose to feel small when I stand beside the ocean and not take it for granted. All of this happen because of me. We both play a part, and it is your choice to share how you feel if you like. It's my choice not to take it personally because of how you feel. A lot of it has nothing to do with me but I learn to deal with who you are and what you went through.

I choose to love you when things seem so impossible. I choose to be family and remember that we are all individuals. There are days when I am not sure what is going on and why there is so much anger. I must remember that my part is not to overthink it. We are broken people who have issues and some of us rather blame others than face our own mess. I know that I have a choice today and if I pray and trust God, He will show me the way.

I can't make you do anything, but I can honor you for who you are and not try to change you or put my expectations on you. We are adult people and to force a person to do something or make demands on a person that you don't want made on you is so unfair. We each have a right to be respected in our place. We can ask, but to demand that you follow my instructions, unless we were in some type of danger, would be so unfair. It's a choice to treat people the way you want to be treated and to speak in a way to give respect and reverence because each of us deserve it. So don't be surprised when you get what you give. What goes around comes around so give what you want to receive.

You don't have to live up to my image of who I think you are or should be. My choice is to love you, stand beside you, encourage you, believe in and pray for you, and let you know, "Me, too." We hold people in a place in our mind, but we all change and go through things in life that hurt and cause us not to trust or have faith in anyone again, not even ourselves. Sometimes we try to put our expectations on others. We want them to be who we think they are or should be instead of allowing them to become in their own timing. When you help a child to find his voice or encourage him to be better or point him in the right direction, that is good. But you can't force anyone to do anything. We can suggest and talk about things but to be rude, disrespectful, and demanding is unfair. We each have a choice in life and to control another person and the decisions they make is unfair. We should all learn to bloom where we are planted hoping to improve ourselves so that we can encourage others to be better also.

It wasn't always like this, and it is not always easy, but you can find peace in letting go and accepting what you can't change or get back, but make sure you forgive, love, and release. Learn to let go of the things that hurt you. Let go of doubt and living in the past with all the mistakes and failures of that time. Let go of the would'ves and could'ves. What can you do now with what you have? What can you change now if you just use this time to think, pray, and look for the good instead of the worst of everything? Who said it would be easy? If everything were easy, we would all be doing it. Soul-searching is hard because you must be honest with yourself. Then we must learn to think about these things: truth, honesty, just, good report, virtues, and praise.

> **Philippians 4:8 - Finally, brethren, whatsoever things are true, whatsoever things are honest, whatsoever things are just, whatsoever things are pure, whatsoever things are lovely, whatsoever things are of good report; if there be any virtue, and if there be any praise, think on these things.**

It's when we learn how to laugh at ourselves and enjoy the moments in life with family or friends that we often miss. Enjoy a song, a quiet moment in stillness of the night, the sound of the ocean, the coolness of a breeze. Listen to the birds sing. Hear a child laugh or a mother speak. I would hear my mom say, "I been where you are trying to go." I was a child once and she would tell us about the time when she was growing up. It wasn't all good, but you learn how to appreciate the little things in life. Some you remember and some you don't. Just don't forget to inhale and exhale and know that you have another chance to get it right.

After the storm has passed, take the time to watch a squirrel play and gather food. Learn how to appreciate the colors of a red jay or blue jay resting on the fence. Live in appreciation of the beauty and handiwork of God all around us. Things are not as bad as they seem. Yes, bad things happen, but life goes on and there is a second chance.

When you can sit and have the chance to sing or listen to a timeless song when you are looking out over the water or watching the sunset, joy rises in your spirit. "Then sings my soul, my savior, God, to thee, how great thou art." God put a rainbow in the sky. It has a way of changing your view if you allow it. You can heal from the hurt and what disappointed you doesn't seem as important.

So, it didn't turn out like I hoped, but I have a choice. I can hide behind the mask of shame or a lifestyle that's out of control, hide from the disappointment of rejection and the feeling of being unloved. But I have a choice in life, and it is the decisions and choices I make that are life changing and long lasting. Make the choice to be happy in your own unique way. Give and live your best life trusting God to guide you through the minefields and don't stay in the place of doubt. Allow yourself to enjoy life, singing songs you choose.

IN THE ROOM AGAIN

Let the word of Christ dwell in you richly in all wisdom; teaching and admonishing one another in psalms and hymns and spiritual songs, singing with grace in your hearts to the Lord. Colossians *3:16* KJ Bible

Here I am again, sitting and pondering, sometimes feeling lonely, wondering what will happen or how will this play out because you don't want to talk. The sound of me breathing and the hum of the fans and the notification bell on my phone makes the silence less deafening, along with the TV.

I sit in silence, replaying the scenes over and over in my head. Feelings of fear and rejection grip me, and I am not sure why. I am sure that anger can be dangerous if it is not controlled and sometimes, I ask the question: why am I here?

I hide because I don't want anyone to know what is going on and sharing what I feel is out of the question. There are times I feel ashamed and not sure if I can go through this again. Part of me wants to scream out loud, asking the questions: Do you see me? Do you understand that I am for you, not against you?

At times, life seems to unravel and I feel as if I need to be less of who I am for you and the question I ask myself is why. When you devalue me, you are devaluing yourself also so why would you settle for half of what is to be whole? It is not about fault or blame and the show of emotion is okay. I have cried more tears than I want and still you don't seem to understand. When life serves you lemons, you make lemonade and crying because of hurt frustration or pain happens when things are not working out the way you want. Life happens. Just keep living.

I watch a movie that I don't really see to keep from thinking because the thoughts in my mind plagues me so. I want better. I want more than we have but I am unsure how to reach it. I never learn to trust because past experiences hold me captive, thinking everyone will do what someone else did that hurt me. But here I am in the room again, the room of my mind, replaying past hurts, disappointment, and pain, making it fit my now. When I'm out I feel no one will know that I'm wearing a mask to hide what is on the inside of me. I hope no one will ever know that life seems most miserable and out of reach. On the inside I am broken, hurting, trying to hold on, always reaching but never able to attain what I am reaching for. The freedom that I want to experience in being free to be me tends to be just out of reach.

I guess I'll pray. I hope God will hear me again and show me the way. LORD, here I am again, hiding, hoping no one will know that I feel lost and miserable. I pray you will help me with the discomfort and show me how to face myself in the mirror. Thank you for healing me and giving me another chance each day to get it right. LORD God, please help me with this. I need you and please speak to me and show me the way. LORD, help my unbelief.

REBUILDING THE WALL/FAMILY RELATIONSHIP

¹⁷Then said I unto them, Ye see the distress that we are in, how Jerusalem lieth waste, and the gates thereof are burned with fire: come, and let us build up the wall of Jerusalem, that we be no more a reproach. ¹⁸Then I told them of the hand of my God which was good upon me; as also the king's words that he had spoken unto me. And they said, Let us rise up and build. So they strengthened their hands for this good work. ¹⁹But when Sanballat the Horonite, and Tobiah the servant, the Ammonite, and Geshem the Arabian, heard it, they laughed us to scorn, and despised us, and said, What is this thing that ye do? will ye rebel against the king? ²⁰Then answered I them, and said unto them, The God of heaven, he will prosper us; therefore we his servants will arise and build: but ye have no portion, nor right, nor memorial, in Jerusalem. Nehemiah 2:17-20

There is a work that needs to be done in the family. The walls are up but the relationship is in need of repair and there seems to be distress in it going back up. There is division and despair. among us. Many have lost sight of what they wanted, and there seems to be little or no peace anywhere. How do we repair what we don't know when communication is lacking because everyone is walking around offended? How do you teach what you find difficult to explain? We are a lost generation in a world of despair when right is wrong and wrong is right. Then we justify the reason we are wrong. What's a soul to do?

Now you may be asking yourself what kind of wall this is, and why it is down, and how it got down, and how we get it up again? There is a wall of division and indifference. That's the first wall. We are divided in our thoughts in how we process the truth. We are indifferent towards one another. It's about me getting mine and forgetting about you. Offence is running rampant and we're always on guard about everything we say. The truth becomes an issue of hate because it's taken out of the context in which it was spoken or meant by the speaker.

There are different types of walls that have been constructed and this is throughout humanity. When you can get people to come into disagreement with one another and blow it out of proportion that's an issue that happens with people. We have walls that keep us separated and the mindset of indifference that says 'it's not my business', and 'it's not happening to me.' We have the walls of unrest, fear, and lack of education. We have no father in the home. Single, pregnant, or unwed mothers try to do it on their own. There seems to be no peace in this life. There is turmoil and addiction, fighting a broken system and ourselves to stay alive. These walls are in many families and someone must be willing to say 'it stops here right now' and repair the breach.

We live in a world where you can go faster, talk faster in multiple ways, and the ability to talk using a phone or computer to see one another. You're not in the same state or room yet we have walls that keep us separated from each other and the truth. We have walls in our mind called subjective thinking. It hinders our relationship, and some think we're doing what's right for our own self. These walls are of a negative state. It's not to build us but to kill us, to keep us divided and down.

Nehemiah was rebuilding the wall of the city. It was about protection. It was constructed to keep the enemy out. The wall in our family needs to be repaired. When you look around at the hopelessness and decay of the family unit, what happened to compassion and grace? Now if this doesn't bother you, then it will stay in ruin until someone has a heart of compassion and begins to weep and cry for what is lost.

The word tells us Nehemiah wept about the ruins and disarray, that no one would rebuild the wall. Now this doesn't mean you won't come up against conflict. You will. It doesn't mean there won't be those who want you to stop. They will, but you will need a made-up mind and a whatever-it-takes attitude. Nothing will stop me from reaching out to the lost and hurting among the ruins. Decide to extend grace because it is extended to us daily. Extend mercy because his mercy is new every morning.

The word tells us that it is the LORD's mercies that we are not consumed and he gives us new mercies and new grace for each new day, I don't look like what I've been through. I'll encourage and love you with the Word. I'll extend my hand to help repair and rebuild because that's what Jesus is doing for me. This is the face of a new generation and he that loves us, gives us overwhelming victories in all these difficulties.

FOLLOW ME

And as Jesus passed forth from thence, he saw a man, named Matthew, sitting at the receipt of custom: and he sayeth unto him, Follow me. And he arose and followed him. Matthew 9:9

I sat waiting to hear a word that I could hold on to. I needed a word that would make me feel better. I read the passage again then I waited for him to speak to me. I read another passage because I desired change and I wanted it to start with me. I thought about the message that I had heard that I am crucified with Christ. I live yet it's not I but Christ who lives in me. Then I heard it: 'follow me.'

> **I am crucified with Christ: nevertheless, I live; yet not I, but Christ liveth in me: and the life which I now live in the flesh I live by the faith of the Son of God, who loved me, and gave himself for me. Galatians 2:20(KJV)**

We often say "I am doing the best I can but I just can't do anymore," but you can. It's in changing the way we see ourselves and the way we think and process what is going on. Now you may wonder what is wrong with the way I think or the way I process or think of myself. The first thing is the I disease. That's half the problem right there. I don't think. That's right. I didn't think to ask the Father. The Word lets us know that we must be sold out for we are a new creature in Christ. We left the old way behind, and all things are becoming new.

Therefore, if any man be in Christ, he is a new creature: old things are passed away; behold, all things are become new. 2 Corinthians 5:17

As I played this over in my mind I wanted to know where I got off track. What happened? I needed to get this right. The answer is life. You see, it doesn't always march by the beat of my or your drum, nor does it turn out the way I want it to because there is more than just me who's involved. I let little things slip in to trip me up and one word turns into a plethora of trivialities. I should have been living by faith and not my flesh because instead of getting frustrated I would have prayed and laid it at the feet of Jesus. But I held on to it and allowed it to get to me. Now that I recognize the problem, I can no longer try and handle it myself. I must lay it at the feet of Jesus, and pick up my cross and follow him.

To be crucified with Christ is important because you recognize that it's not you and you don't have to handle every little problem, and I don't have to allow everything to work my nerves. The Word of God must have room to work on me in the midst of whatever is going on in my life. I can't be new if I continue to allow the old stuff that I said I gave to God to have free course to rise whenever it felt like it. I can't allow the enemy room to work. I must keep the Word of God before me, showing me my errors even when I don't like it or want to look at them.

When He says follow me, it's not because he doesn't know that I am a mess. It's because he wants me to be better, to do better, to learn about him as He teaches me. And I can't do it if I am not following Him.

COMPASSION AND ENCOURAGEMENT

My Dear Sister,

We are sisters in the spirit although we have not met. Kaitlyn, I want to speak to your spirit man and encourage you. I hope that you will hear me in the spirit as I speak truth to power and life in you. I pray you relax, breath in deeply, and exhale, then listen with your heart as our Heavenly Father uses the words on these pages to encourage you.

The word of God tells us in Philippians 4:6-7 to be anxious for nothing but in prayer and supplication with thanksgiving we make our request known to God, and the peace of God that surpasses all understanding will guard our hearts and mind in Christ Jesus. Now prayer is a conversation that we have with Papa Daddy and supplication is asking or telling him urgently, earnestly, and humbly what we need. In another portion of scripture, he tells us in everything to give thanks for this is the will of God in Christ Jesus concerning you. This lets me know there is nothing that we are going through in this life that our father isn't concerned about. If it troubles us he wants us to tell him, although he already knows. So don't sit there in distress. The kingdom of God is voice activated. You must open your mouth and talk to him about everything that concerns you. It doesn't matter what it is. Tell him what's in your heart.

I want you to be your own kind of beautiful in your most unique way. I want you to understand that you are fearfully and wonderfully made and your soul knoweth right well. You were made in his image. You are made just like him, and Father God loves you just the way you are. You don't have to prove anything. Just have faith and trust the God in you. Then do the word — act on it by casting all your cares on him because he cares for you. Life is hard and sometimes it dips and here's another trip: too much to do, and not enough time — it seems we run out of time. What's a soul to do? And now you're tired. We run after things trying to do it in our strength and might. Some are over achievers for one reason or another. There is the way we feel about ourselves then there's what we've heard someone say about us.

Now there's a story we tell ourselves. You know what you say to yourself when you are alone and fear brings loneliness because you don't have any friends or you feel left out. All these feelings want to consume our thoughts and emotions. The Word tells us to cast down thoughts and imaginations and every high thing that exalts or comes against the knowledge of God and bring those thoughts into captivity to the obedience of God's word. Then He tells us what to think on whatsoever things are true, honest, just, pure, lovely — if it is good, if there is any virtue, if it is praise worthy. Think about these things according to Philippian 4:8. We must say what He says about us and not what we think. Then ask Him in prayer to take away the loneliness and put people in our path we need to encourage. You will find joy in life when you allow God to use you to help someone else to be encouraged or overcome a struggle because of what you said to them. It's the experiences we have that help others — to know that it was his grace and mercy that kept you when you would have fainted or given up.

> **22It is of the LORD'S mercies that we are not consumed, because his compassions fail not. 23They are new every morning: great is your faithfulness. 24The LORD is my portion, says my soul; therefore, will I hope in him. Lamentations 3:22-24 KJV**

There are many things in life that we will face — some difficult and some very painful — but you will survive because that's what you do. We will accept the fact that all of us will not be a size 5, 10, or 12. Some of us are thick, beautiful and smart. You, Kaitlyn, have value and I want you to know your self-worth. You're worth it because God sent his only son to die for you. You are worth it because if it had been no one else He would have done it for you. I want you to know that you're worth saving, keeping, healing and you are worth the sacrifice. You, Kaitlyn, as a strong woman have the power to change the atmosphere when you walk into a room, because you got it like that. You know who you are, and to whom you belong. You may wonder why I am telling you this. I have faced the same things and I have a daughter that has had her struggles in life also but God is faithful.

When you come to a place and you don't know anyone there — there is no family or old friends — do the will of the God and follow your dreams because they come from Him and there is something in your spirit that pushes you to keep moving even if circumstance seems to be against you. There are days you're not sure and it seems like all of hell has come against you. What do you do? We keep moving. His spirit will not send you where his grace can't keep you.

He delivers us when we call out to him in our distress. He moves on our behalf and delivers us. You are not alone, Kaitlyn. All you have to do is ask the Father in His Son's name and tap into the power that's on the inside of you. He will give you all you need for the journey, and He will walk with you every step of the way.

I know He will because He is doing it for me and my children. We must be willing to perservere beyond our discomfort and circumstance that seem to overwhelm us, and press into Him, allowing his mercy and grace to help us face discouragement.

While letting the circumstances know I am not defeated and I won't back down God oversees my life, and all that concerns me are in his hands he can handle it and it won't catch him by surprise. We must determine within ourselves that we will. Live like you are Loved because we are not beggars asking for scraps of anything his strength is made prefect in my weakness. My daddy is the King and that makes me royalty, and we will Live Bold because he instructs me and teaches me the way I should go, and he counsels me with his eye upon me.

Because he that loves us gives us overwhelming victories in all these difficulties. Romans 8:37 GW translation

Tamie S. Johnson

HEALING FOR A HEART

Hello Gabby,

I know you don't know me but consider me a sister that you haven't met. I want to speak to your heart and the pain you must feel and the process of healing a heart that's heavy. I know that it is hard right now and you may wonder if this hurt will ever stop…. it will. It may not be today but one day it won't hurt nearly as bad as it does right now. Sometimes you will have doubts and fears whether you will ever get past all of this …. you will. I say it with all the confidence I have in God who loves you and He will strengthen you as you go through this.

You may wonder if anyone understands how you feel right now and if you are a believer, you may even question if God cares. The answer is yes. Yes, He does and there is someone who understands how you may be feeling at this point in your life. I know that God cares because His word says that He is our faithful high priest who knows what we are going through. God understands our pain because He sent his only Son to die for humanity. Now that may sound a little preachy to you, but I want you to understand that God loves you and He sees your pain.

> **Fear not, for I am with you; be not dismayed, for I am your God; I will strengthen you, I will help you, I will uphold you with my righteous right hand. Isaiah 41:10**

There's a young lady who got pregnant at a young age and she lost that baby. She thought the sun would never shine again, nor would she be able to smile again. It was her intent to give all the love and attention to that little one that she was carrying but it didn't happen for her. She lost that baby. The hardest part was to go through the same delivery process as if she would bring him home. I spent a lot of time crying. It seemed to be one of the hardest things I ever had to endure but one day it didn't hurt as bad.

Notice I said 'as bad' not 'it didn't hurt.' My mom told me, "Baby you will smile again and you won't feel as sad as you do right now. We come in this world, and we are on our way out. We sometimes have the experience of carrying a life inside of us but it's not his/her time for one reason or another. But we learn as we go that time and life is in Gods had and man can't give life that comes from God. You may not understand right now but in time you will. Mom told me He is too wise to make a mistake and He is too just to do wrong. We can't see the end from the beginning. He can, and we don't know the road that's ahead. You can talk to Him and ask Him to help you bear it. He already knows how you feel but He wants a conversation with you. And you can cast all the pain, disappointments, hurt and tears at His feet because He cares for you."

⁷Casting all your care upon him; for he careth for you. 1 Peter 5:7KJV

Pain is very uncomfortable, and it is something we spend a lot of time trying to avoid but it's something we all face in this life, and we must feel it to heal it. That's an invitation for God to come in and replace our faltering strength with His strength. Because His strength is made perfect in our weakness. It's ok to cry and sometimes you may have a moment or two, but you'll get through it. It's natural for you to mourn the loss of your child acknowledge the fact that it does hurt and trust that it will get better in time.

And this is the confidence that we have toward him, that if we ask anything according to his will he hears us. 1 John 5:14

One of life's antibiotic is to believe even when life feels like it's falling apart. That may be a question in your mind. Believe what? That it will get better. You are not alone. You are loved. Someone cares. Talk to Him. Start laying it at the feet of the Father. It will be ok. and you will be okay, too. Earth has no sorrow that heaven can't heal. We don't see it while we are going through it, but the sun will shine again.

The LORD is a stronghold for the oppressed, a stronghold in times of trouble. And those who know your name put their trust in you, for you, O LORD, have not forsaken those who seek you. Psalms 9:9

HE CALLED YOU BEAUTIFUL

Fear ye not therefore, ye are of more value than many sparrows. Matthew 10:31

How much then is a man better than a sheep? Wherefore it is lawful to do well on the Sabbath days. Matthew 12:12

When is it ok to treat me as if I'm less than human? I'm different in some countries. They are call untouchable people Dalit. They are a broken, downtrodden, and oppressed people and they have no hope or dreams for their future, for things to get better in their life. The society they live in has beaten them and they believe the lie that has been told to them. They feel helpless when their daughters are raped and murdered and no one seems to care. I am untouchable — a Dalit.

When you leave or escape the cruelty of a society where you live and try to start over again it becomes hard because you have been told this all your life — that you are not worthy or haven't the right of human dignity. You see people treated worse than animals. In fact, animals are given more respect than you as a human. You are considered nothing more than the filth of the earth, only worthy of cleaning up someone else's dung and waste without proper protection. How do you pick your head up after this? How do you give your children hope when they are born into this? You're raped and degraded. You're not good enough to be treated as well as a prostitute. That is the fate of some women in Asia, India, and other surrounding countries.

Now I have escaped and I'm in another place, but I'm still trapped by the thoughts that are in my mind and what has been said to me and about me. I know what the Word says but still I feel unworthy. It's meant for someone else. I can believe for someone else but can't believe for me and I cry inside because I'm trapped in my mind with what's been said to me and the stories that I tell myself.

The word of God says that I am fearfully and wonderful made and He calls me his beloved. His Word tells me that I am worth more than any sparrow and I am better than the animals but somehow, I miss this when it comes to me. I walk in fear that someone will hurt me because I was told that I was ugly. After hearing it so long, I believe it. Although I know that I am not a mistake, I feel that I am and I have no value and it's not true.

How do I live loved when my whole being is so unloved? How do I trust that He is with me when I still believe the lie that was told to me? Everyone else sees beauty in me and all I see is ugliness and fear.

Dear God, if you can hear, please help me. Deliver me from the lie that plagues my thoughts. Help me to cast all my cares on you. Teach me how to think of the things that are praiseworthy, virtuous, and of a good report. —to say what you say about me and not the lie I believed about myself. Renew my mind in your Word that I will hear you. Father, keep me in your care that I do not run for fear. Thank you for hearing me. AMEN.

Ida, I know you don't believe what the enemy has told you because you are a powerful woman in the word of God. When we repeat what God said, it cancels out what the enemy says and every lie that has been told to you. I want you to live loved, trusting God and repeat to yourself, 'I am made in His image. I am made just like Him, I have the attributes of my Father. His word says I am fearfully and wonderfully made, and my soul knows right well.' God did not make any junk and I am adopted. I am a royal priesthood and a holy nation. I am a part of the Kingdom of God. Everything my God made is good and very good and when he made you, he called you beautiful. And you are precious in his eyes.

TAILOR-MADE FOR THIS

Before she walked out, she gave herself the once over in her full-length mirror — turning this way and that, making sure all is in place, smiling to herself, knowing it was a journey, but God's grace and mercy kept her. This thought came to her mind; my this may not be your this, the things that I struggled with aren't the same as yours. There may be a correlation — different place, different time and related in one way or another.

Praise be to God. I know who I am, and I don't look like what I've been through. When a sister hears your story, she says, 'Yes! She made it and I can too.' She believed for us and with us. I believe her. She had to win this battle and survive, because it wasn't for her — it was for us. We are the ones she has pulled up, held up, helped up, and carried. We are the ones she prayed through difficult times. No, it wasn't easy and there were days I felt like giving up, and every time I fell, I cried, and I looked up and prayed. Many days there will be tears. You must learn to encourage yourself, telling yourself, 'I'm built for this.' I am one amongst many that have survived hardships, abuse, insults, rejection, abandonment, and derogatory verbiage, to name a few. I stand on the shoulders of praying women, prayer warriors, and intercessors who made it possible for me to be here today.

You see, the enemy thought he had me. He was sure I would give up, and he was sure he had won. There was something he couldn't see. It's in the inside of me. On me it could get washed off, or knocked off but this, you can't see with the natural eye. You may see me fall but you didn't see when Jesus picked me up. The haters couldn't understand why I didn't give up or quit but they didn't know my value, nor could they ascertain my worth. The Devil fooled himself into thinking that if he hit hard enough I would just fold. No! That's not the hand I hold.

I know who I am and whose I am. I was made in his image I was made just like Him. He said I am fearfully and wonderfully made and my soul knoweth right well. He said I am the head and not the tail — above only never beneath. I am blessed going out and coming in. I am blessed in the city, blessed in the field. My store house is blessed, and while the earth remains seedtime and harvest, cold and heat, summer and winter, day and night shall not cease. I walk blessed. I talk blessed. I am blessed to be a blessing.

What the enemy didn't know is I am a vessel full of power. The word tells me we are troubled on every side but not in distress, perplexed but not in despair, persecuted, but not forsaken, cast down but not destroyed. I've had some painful circumstances, but his grace and mercy are with me every day and prayer keeps me standing. I am a treasure who can't be compared. I am a vessel full of power and a presentation of a shapely shade of power. I'm tailor-made for this.

> **"Now unto him that is able to keep you from falling, and to present you faultless before the presence of his glory with exceeding joy," Jude 1:24**

A Presentation of perfectly Shapely Shades of Power.

LIVING IT: SAVED, SASSY, AND SIXTY

A virtuous woman *is* a crown to her husband: but she that maketh ashamed *is* as rottenness in his bones Proverbs 12:4

Before she walked out, she gave herself the once over in her full-length mirror. Turning this way and that, making sure all is in place — smiling to herself, knowing it as it should be for her soul knoweth right well. She is a virtuous woman and a crown to her husband, family, and friends. She's not defined by the events that has happened in her life. Truth be told, we've all had some painful circumstances. To be a shapely shade of power and authority doesn't happen by chance. She's proud but not prideful, intelligent, poised, and full grace. She has learned at the feet of a Queen, the matriarch that has poured into her. Mrs. Otis Belle Meyers is her name.

It's not enough to just be, you must be about it living it walking it out daily because someone is watching you.

She is rare, and her price is far above diamonds or rubies and if she imitates, she imitates the one who came before, the one who taught her. This doesn't just happen. It comes with a price. You learn it on your knees, praying in the spirit. This doesn't mean she's superwoman who hasn't made mistakes. She prays, "Lord keep me humble. Help me to be what you called me to be, and check my love walk daily. Guide me, give me wisdom, and teach me how to live this life before your people."

It's not about impressing anyone. That would be a mistake, but it's important that you be today who you want to be tomorrow when you face yourself in the mirror.

She's a vessel full of power, a confident shapely shade who knows who she is. She walks in strength and honor. They are her clothing, and she is not fearful of the future or trouble. She is the keeper of dreams that brings about hope. She's whole, complete, and she is the incubator who holds his dreams.

She encourages, motivates, and builds, and the crown placed on her head doesn't tilt or lean precariously. Her confidence is not in the outward, adoring. She does look good, but it's what's on the inside of her. She was left a legacy to carry forward, to build up and speak life to us. Today we stand and applaud you and we say Happy Birthday.

LOOKING FOR MYSELF

Something or someone is chasing me and recording the things I do and speak. I feel that it is looking into my past. This discomfort causes me to remember things about me I thought I had put away. I find myself looking for me — the me that I want to get to know the me that has value and purpose and untapped potential. I find myself looking for a plan that was written before my birth. Now my mind seems overworked although I find that life is interesting and very complex.

I often find myself chasing a dollar, trying to work things out on my own, telling myself this will help me to feel better. Girl, keep it moving. Make yourself looking good and be happy and keep doing you, whatever that is. My plans don't often work out the way I hope they will. Oftentimes, I miss the most important person in all of this, sitting here looking back over my life and I wonder what happened. How did I get to this place? I go to work and church but not really living. I know something's missing. The older church folk would say "Child, you're living beneath your privilege, honey. Child, you're not trusting God. He's the one who has the answers to your questions, and you avoid asking Him because of the thoughts in your mind. I Look for ways to self-validate, searching for something to tell me who I am. I often ask where I go from here. One day this scripture came to my mind:

Proverbs 3:5-8 ⁵Trust in the LORD with all thine heart; and lean not unto thine own understanding. ⁶In all thy ways acknowledge him, and he shall direct thy paths. ⁷Be not wise in thine own eyes: fear the LORD, and depart from evil. ⁸It shall be health to thy navel, and marrow to thy bones.

You are doing all you can. You never ask God. You're trusting in your ability with limited knowledge. You can't fix it. You repeat the lie: you're not good enough or smart enough. You ask why God won't help you with this, but you fail to ask Him.

Psalms 3 But thou, O LORD, art a shield for me; my glory, and the lifter up of mine head. ⁴I cried unto the LORD with my voice, and he heard me out of his holy hill.

There is hope and He hears me when I call to Him, I'm learning that it's a process. It is not instant. I have questions that I can't answer right now, but it will come. I often find myself in a struggle, looking for myself, searching for who I am.

What is His plan for my life? I struggle with surrendering everything to God. There's a part of me that I keep to myself and I wonder why. He knows everything. I can't protect me from life. It's in living life that you will experience joy and pain alike. Love and life arenot the absents of pain. I can't protect me from anything. I don't have the power to control situations when life happens. So what keeps me holding back when I just want to let go? I ask the real me who wants better, to end this struggle to get my life right, and stand on my feet, start living like I know I am trusting in the one who set me free.

1 Peter 5:7 (KJV) ⁷Casting all your care upon him; for he careth for you.

Rejoice in hope, be patient in tribulation, be constant in prayer. **Romans 12:12**

MS. SHARON K
STRENGTH AND HONOR

Strength and honour are her clothing; and she shall rejoice in time to come. Proverbs 31:25 KJV

Thinking about my life and going over things in my mind, what does the future hold and where do I go from here? I am reminded of the Word:

> **10But he knoweth the way that I take: when he hath tried me, I shall come forth as gold. Job 23:10**

There is brokenness, rejection, abandonment, and pain. Still there's potential and hope. Starting over is not bad depending on one's perspective. It's a new season in life where change takes place. Before she walked out, she gave herself the once over in her full-length mirror — turning this way and that, making sure all is well smiling to herself, knowing it is what it is, and her soul knoweth right well. A Virtuous woman is not defined by the events that has happened in her life. Life happens to all of us. Truth be told, we've all had some painful circumstances and to be a Godly woman of power and authority doesn't happen by chance.

She's proud, but not prideful, intelligent, poised, and she has grace. We need that. She often reminds herself what the Word says about her because He knows what lies before her.

......[17] For our light affliction, which is but for a moment, worketh for us a far more exceeding and eternal weight of glory; I know the plans that I have for you, declares the LORD. They are plans for peace and not disaster, plans to give you a future filled with hope. Jeremiah 29:11 GWT

Then she reminds herself [14]For he performeth *the thing that is* appointed for me: and many such *things are* with him. Job 23:10,14 KJ

It's not enough to be. You must be intentional about it — living it, and walking it out daily. Someone is watching and wants to be like you. This doesn't just happen to you. It comes with a price.

Stand in the face of adversity when everything in you screams and cries out in the midst of it all as you learn on your knees in prayer, having faith trusting God, and praying in the spirit. This doesn't mean trouble hasn't made an appearance in your life, nor does it mean you haven't made mistakes. It doesn't mean that you are super strong, and nothing bothers you. She knows who she is. She's an intercessor who's been called. She stands on the shoulders of prayer warriors and intercessors who lifted her up and prayed her through before she knew how.

Now she stands in the gap and makes up the hedge, and she is always willing to encourage and pray for you. While praying for others, she prays for herself: 'Lord keep me humble, check my love walk, help me to be what you're calling me to be, guide and order my steps. Lord give me wisdom and teach me how to live this life before people.'

You learn everyone you meet or interact with is not always for you or against you. Sometimes they just don't know any better. Don't take it personally. It's not about you. Impressing anyone would be a mistake. It's important that you be today who you want to be tomorrow when you face yourself in the mirror. You want to be a vessel full of power, to be a confident woman who discerns in the spirit, knowing change will come and that it is necessary in life. Strength and honor are her clothing, and she is not fearful of the future or trouble. Her desire is to walk in integrity and honor Him.

Seasons change. We, the people, must also change. It's important to prepare and be prepared. Just because you leave one station doesn't mean you're done. She has the tenacity to keep moving forward. Fear tries to come in, but it can't stay. She reminds herself of the Word. He has not given me a spirit of fear but love, power and a sound mind. Life and love can be painful and joyful. She's a woman of God who knows there is much to do, and to whom much is given, much is required so she carries on.

She knows as she stands on the shoulders of prayer warriors and intercessors who lifted her in prayer and annihilated the plan of the enemy in the spirit before it happens. Now she teaches others to bind and loose and annihilate and come against illicit lifestyles and traps of the enemy. She is leaving a legacy for others to follow as she continues to pray, living a life that she was tailor-made to live.

RING THE BELL

⁹Remember the former things of old: for I am God, and there is none else; I am God, and there is none like me; ¹⁰declaring the end from the beginning, and from ancient times things that are not yet done; saying, My counsel shall stand, and I will do all my pleasure; Isaiah 46:9-10

There are things we want to remember and there are things that we want to forget. We remember the good times verses the bad times, then we compare the two. We blame or make excuses for behaviors and for what happened at that time. There are things in life that we should never use as a comparison because they will not measure up. God told the children to forget the former things. Don't try to compare it to your now. There is a greater glory now than then and know two trials are the same. He is the same God but what He did in the last events or years can't be compared to what He will do in this year, this time.

So it is with us in relationships and life, past and present. We should go from good to better then best and stop comparing because we changed in those situations. Change is what you want and what brought you to that place will change because you should mature and grow up in your thinking. You can't blame everyone else forever and never take responsibility for yourself, for your actions — what you said or did.

There is an expectation on the inside that causes you to strive for a better understanding to improve attitudes and mindsets, to be better, striving for more to get what you want. When you achieve it, you can say it wasn't easy. There was a cost to get here, but it was worth it to get to this place. You must ring the bell. For you, living life will cost you something, If it doesn't cost you anything, there is no value in it.

When you see someone go through a traumatic experience or treatment and can tell you about it without bitterness, they have succeeded and have rung the bell. This is to acknowledge that accomplishment. I made it. This is not to say that the person that did not ring the bell failed. It means the bell tolled for them in a different way. They have the chance to rest or try again or just be free from labor and pain. Still, much was accomplished while they were in the fight, and they fought a good fight prayerfully, holding on to faith to receive their reward.

Now on this side when we remember the fight, we remember what was endured to get to the place of I-made-it. The bell may not be a physical bell, but it is the feeling of satisfaction you get when you know that you did your best. It was hard, but with the help of God, you made it. When you get the knockout after the count of ten, and the opponent doesn't get up, they ring the bell. The victor raises his hands, jumping up and down, knowing it was a difficult fight, but he made it to the end on his feet. It wasn't his strength that kept him or allowed him to stand, His grace and mercy is the reason.

What I went through then can't be compared to what I am going through now. Then, there wasn't much wisdom. I thought I was doing it for myself, but my wisdom couldn't save me or keep me from going through. It is in the things we suffer that teaches us. In the scripture, Job said, "Many such things are appointed to me but when he has tried me, I shall come forth as pure gold."

If we never have a test, there is no crown. If we never go through hard times or have troubles in life, we never learn to appreciate the good when it happens. Look back at the hard times and tell him thank you. Because you didn't leave me where I was, now you have allowed me to see how I got over on the other side. It wasn't the sinking but His outstretched hand that kept me from drowning in the midst of it. It's where God brought you from that gives you a reason to ring the bell. The old saints would say, 'give him praise.' It's not remembering the bad but knowing how to praise in the midst of it because He isn't finished yet. The word tells us in all things, give thanks for this is the will of God in Christ Jesus concerning you.

1 Thessalonians 5:18—In everything give thanks: for this is the will of God in Christ Jesus concerning you.

Colossians 3:17—And whatsoever ye do in word or deed, do all in the name of the Lord Jesus, giving thanks to God and the Father by him.

Psalms 107:1—O give thanks unto the LORD, for he is good: for his mercy endureth forever.

If you haven't rung the bell, you should try it. Recall how far you have come in the face of a pandemic. Remember the things that you were kept from by this pandemic. If it didn't kill you there is a reason to praise Him for the things you learned. Some felt they could not last but if you live to see another day, that is a reason to ring the bell. There were many who reconnected with their children. Some learned to cook instead of eating fast food. There were some who lost weight and got healthy. To ring the bell in this life is a good thing if you learned anything about yourself and what you want. There was no physical bell when Israel went through the red sea and ate manna while going to their promise land. Their clothes and shoes didn't wear out. God kept them safe and made provisions for them, and he has done so for us. It wasn't our wisdom, and our arm could not save us but we have been given another chance to thank him right where we are. Ring the bell.

F YOU
#FORGIVEYOU #FORGIVEME
#FORGIVETHEM

Be kind to one another, tenderhearted, forgiving one another, as God in Christ forgave you. Ephesians 4:32

You want respect but are never able to give it because it was you who was hurt. It was you who was let down. Everyone let you down and you had to do everything on your own.

Untapped potential, misunderstanding, unmet expectations — no one understands how you feel. You have been mistreated all your life, you say. Why is it so hard for you to be understanding and treat people the way you want to be treated? I often ask this question, but I never get a real answer. You use excuses to hold others hostage because you were hurt. Now it is in your mind that everyone will hurt you, disappoint you, and let you down. If they are not, you make sure something is up so you can feel better about how you are feeling.

Most times it is better for me to walk away from the disagreement and allow a person time to cool off because I want to be fair. I don't want to say something I can't take back. It is better than standing there trying to explain what you really don't want to hear. You will twist my words to fit what you want it to be. So to avoid confusion, I walk away.

After listening to the same put-downs, shouting, and name-calling, kindergarten behavior gets old. You wonder if they will ever grow up and stop the woe-is-me that has not changed in twelve years. It's all about you and your hurt, let downs, and disappointments that haven't been dealt with and you act as if you are okay. You hurt someone or disappointed someone also, but you won't let it touch you. Why all the drama with the hurt feelings, trying to hit below the belt!

Life is full of disappointments to allow you to see where you are. It's the mirror of the soul but how you process all of this is important because you must be honest with yourself. When you are not honest with yourself and your behavior, it's like drinking poison expecting different results. You can't hold everyone hostage because you were hurt at one point in life. It is not new. Everyone has been hurt, let down, or disappointed at some point in time and it's not everyone's fault. A person must be willing to forgive and move forward. Learn the lesson that is before you and forgiveness is a must. Life is a series of lessons and tests and how well we get through it determines our growth, maturity, and how we handle conflict.

Some of us act like children, wanting our way, but who are you willing to forgive for making a mistake or forgetting because life happens. It's part of the process. However, when the tide turns, you want what you are not willing to give. Making accusations that are partly true or not true at all and being ugly just because you are in your feelings. Get over it. F you. Forgive yourself. Forgive others. Forgive me. Everyone deserves understanding, mercy, and grace. It is being willing to extend this to everyone and putting past failures and behaviors behind us.

It never ceases to amaze me how one wrong is so small and it is supposed to be overlooked and forgiven immediately. It was you. It was you who didn't know. It was you who forgot. It was you who said it didn't matter. But you want forgiveness, and you want the other person to move on and put it behind them. Forgive me, Forgive you. Life is not the absence of pain and if you live, you will experience both and forgiveness is the key to healing and reconciliation, It is hard to be big when littles has you. So, F you! #forgiveyou #forgiveme.

PERSPECTIVE AND ANGER

What is perspective and why is it important? Is it about convincing another person to think as I think? Or is it just the way we see things as individuals? Webster's dictionary says: the interrelation in which a subject or its parts are mentally viewed; of, relating to, employing, or seen in perspective. I believe we see things differently. It's like the blind men with the elephant. Each one saw it differently although they could not physically see it. So it is with life. Each of us has a different point of view, position, posture. I understand each of us is different but although we were raised by the same person, hearing the same thing, we all perceive things differently. This causes us to change our view as we get older due to relationships, peer pressure and other outside influences. We tend to think that what we were taught as a child is outdated and old-fashioned. This finds us in a place of moral decay. We wonder why things are the way they are now. We have little to no respect for each other, nor for the people who raised us up. We look with disdain as if it's an insult for an older person to tell you something. The hair on their head is grey. They didn't get there without learning something. There has been love, sickness and pain, disappointments and let downs, but they made it and can tell you something.

Why is there so much anger in the world and why do we blow up at the smallest things? What is the real reason we're angry? It can't be what was said to us and if we know who we are, why let that enter our heart and cause us such discomfort.? I don't understand that. Webster's dictionary explains it like this: a strong feeling of displeasure and usually of antagonism, anger, ire, rage, fury, indignation, wrath mean an intense emotional state induced by displeasure. anger, the most general term, names the reaction but by itself does not convey cause or intensity. ire, more frequent in literary contexts, suggests an intense anger, often with an evident display of feeling. I don't understand. As we get older, we should understand anger and emotional display doesn't change anything. If we know who we are then we should be able to reason with one another unless we want to control or manipulate the situation to our advantage. We all see things differently and we can be visibly upset without all the others, anger, ire, rage, fury, and indignation, coming into play. We allow our emotions to get out of control and all these other baggage. I can be hurt without being angry. I can be upset without being angry. I can just be disappointed. We spend our life trying to keep life a secret. We don't want to talk about our life. It is personal and it's not that other people can benefit from our experiences. I'm not saying we must say everything that happens in our house, but we can be wise about our life experiences and until we learn to talk about what has happened and tap into the root of the anger, we will spin our wheels running from things instead of dealing with it. I try not to get angry. No, I am not perfect and sometimes I miss it but I often try to understand and see it from a different perspective. I pray that God will give me understanding and foresight not to expel energy being upset about something we can work out. I have been there and it's not a nice place to be and I don't like losing control. In that state of mind, we are not capable of sound judgement to make a wise decision because our emotions are in the way. Trying to decide something while upset is not good because when we look back, we find that we over-reacted. The Word tells us that anger lies in the bosom of fools, and I don't want to be a fool.

Be not hasty in thy spirit to be angry: for anger resteth in the bosom of fools. (KJV) Ecclesiastes7:9

My prayer is for my family and children to tap into the source of anger. What is the root of the problem? Why does it upset you? Why are you over the top angry and how do you solve it? Finding it difficult to talk in a calm and rational state without blowing up and coming out of character is not a good thing. We should be able to find out the motive behind the action without division. I find myself in the valley of decision, often crying out to God to help me with this. I don't want the past sins to keep coming back home, spreading its evil disdain for peace in the life of my family. We must deal with our past hurts and disappointments. We must stop blaming others and look at it for what it is. If it's a decision you made out of anger, deal with it. I don't want my children to have to deal with what I refused to deal with.

When we look in the word of God, Abraham had a problem in his house. King David had a problem in his house and many others. King David's father had a problem that he had not overcome so now it falls to the sons. Now, David is no longer the shepherd boy. He is King and there is a problem in his house he didn't deal with it and now he is running from his son. We must deal with life situations that come up. We can't continue to sweep it under the rug, side-stepping it or ignoring the elephant in the room, so to speak. It is required of us to be wise as serpents and harmless as doves. Yes, evil resides in the world but you don't have to partake of it.

God is faithful. He was obedient enough to die on the cross for us. Can't we get it together to stop the senseless display of emotional anger and ire? We want to leave a Godly heritage for our children, not leaving them to try and figure out where this came from and why this happened to them. Life happens to all of us and if we continue, we will have disappointments, hurts and pain with a letdown or two, but it is how you choose to handle the situation or allow the situation to handle you. I pray you choose well and allow God to guide you in this.

YOU DIDN'T KNOW

I'm not sure I understand what you are saying. What are you talking about? Are you saying you didn't know the position you asked for, and what it entailed to be my husband and for me to be your wife? You didn't know the cost of sharing your life or what you may have to give up? you didn't know? what? You didn't know you would have to compromise, and share your time? You didn't know as a husband, a man, that marriage requires you to lead, not dictate, encourage and build up, not boss around?

You're telling me you didn't know that you were to be the provider, the head, the priest of the home? Now you feel like you are the only one who will make decisions and decide about our life. I am not sure I understand your posture, your position. What you're saying doesn't make sense to me. You say because you were married once, that makes you the authority. Look, Honey, my stand is this: just because you did it once does not make you the authority. There are many who repeat a grade, but if you never apply the principles that was taught or required to learn you are just repeating, going over the same old stuff and learning nothing from past mistakes. We must work on correcting what's wrong. You know the old saying, "Do what you've always done and you will get what you have always had."

What you didn't know is that relationships are built. They don't just fall from the sky. It takes two people with time for each other no matter what is going on in your life. You didn't know that we all experience pain and just because you are hurting, life doesn't stop. You didn't know what was required of you as a husband, a friend. It's not that you are in the dark or left out. You refuse to listen or try and understand. I told you what I wanted. I didn't leave you out.

I'm trying to wrap my mind around this and make sense of what's going on. The stance that you are taking doesn't make sense to me. You live as if you are the only one with pain or has suffered loss. You act as if you're the only one with worries. It doesn't matter about anyone else. It's all about you and your dogs. We are supposed to be one, not divided in this but I get the feeling you're drawing a line and daring me to cross because you feel you are the authority.

Now I understand that we are all different, and everyone handles things differently, but you are angry at the wrong one. It wasn't me. I did nothing to you, but you are angry. You don't trust me, but you say you love me. Something is wrong here. You talk about what everyone else has done to you and you're ready to hand out blame, but you never take any for yourself. You say you're hurt but you won't talk, Walking around pouting and cussing folk out as if that explains things. Will it change anything? I'm afraid it won't.

When I try to talk with you, it is always about what someone else did to you and how disappointing life has been to you. Then you cuss and call names but can't explain anything. You talk about everyone else except you. Hey, what do you expect and what is it that you want? Now please help me with this because I either missed something or you misunderstood what I said.

There was a time we could talk but now you are hurtful and angry. You are cussing, name calling as if that's who I am, hiding your own lack of moral integrity, not being honest with yourself. You won't face your own failures and fears. Each day you become vile and withdrawn. Every time the tide shifts, it's something new — more suspension, with a judgmental attitude, and criticism. No matter what I try to do, you are not pleased, and you always find something wrong. You say it's my fault half the time. I don't know what you are talking about. What seems to be the problem? I can't say it's your problem because for me we are in this together. Now help me if you will because I want to know.

You used to say I'm sorry but now you've developed this attitude. You don't apologize for anything, or to anyone, because no one ever apologized to you for the pain they have caused you. Now that's crazy to me. I'm not responsible for what anyone else does or say. I'm only responsible for me, since we are adults and not children. Please help me understand this.

Please help me see what any of that has to do with me. I guess it was always about you not me, or did I miss something here.

I guess you didn't know that we all suffer adversity in life because we live in a fallen world where rain falls in everyone's life. We are broken people who are in need of a savior. It doesn't matter what your position, title, or state is. Rich or poor, upper class, or middle, the road life happens to us all. You were not singled out to say it just happened to you. It is misleading and so untrue. Life is not to be lived looking in a rear-view mirror and if that's your perspective, okay, but it's not mine. We must know that God is our anchor in every storm, and it is his anchor that holds, and he will not leave you alone, but you must trust him. We must understand we can't do anything in our own power or strength, but God is able. It is important that we don't let the past hold us captive by looking back at what was. It may have been painful and disappointing, but keeping it in the front or allowing it to control your life now is not the answer. It is important to know that God is faithful even when we are not, and what we go through in life helps to develop our character and makes us better and stronger. A rearview mirror is not the way to live life. Our character is who we are when no one is watching. We must be willing to leave a legacy saying it stops now and our children will be proud after we are gone because we worked at bettering our relationship. We should always aspire to be better than we were before each year, make a change for the better and not leave our children and grandchildren wondering if this lot will fall to them.

Leave something they can aspire to being better, because grandpa and grandma always said to trust God and keep him first and be a little better each day than you were yesterday. That's the hope in my heart, and I'm striving for it. But you didn't know.

LETTING GO WHILE HOLDING ON

Here I am again, saying to myself I am not going through this again. I'm sick and tired of being sick and tired. Just let it go. But a part of me has a grip that must be pried away because of fear of the unknown.

In my mind, I ask the question: is it worth the hell you go through trying to hold on? Is it helpful holding on because you think you can change it? What? You hope he will change because you don't want to feel like you failed — loving someone who does not know your value and can't see your worth.

I am holding on, hoping and praying it gets better, Girl let it go. Why try anymore? This is hard when only one person can see something is wrong. You are the one who is always wrong. When they feel like you are the problem and there is nothing wrong with them. Face the truth: the only person you can change is you. If a person does not appreciate your value, your value will not decrease just because they cannot see it. Learn to pat yourself on the back and say: You go, girl. We got this.

You want to let go but are unsure how because your emotions are all over the place, and your feelings get in the way of being objective. You play it over in your mind, trying to figure out how you came to this place.

I want the situation to change but make excuses for not moving forward because I'm stuck. How do I get through it? It feels like I was betrayed and let down. Before I get to the place of letting go, I must walk through this minefield of questions and stop overthinking with all the self-doubt. I feel as if I am in a game of tug of war, a battle for my soul and spirit. I'm trying to break my will that I will believe the lie. It was all your fault. I am being pulled in many directions, trying not to cross that line. The struggle is real.

A thought came to mind. Let it all go and slip away to another place. Drive off the bridge. Speed up and lose control of the car. HOLD UP! STOP! Wrong turn. WRONG! I thought I had to pump the brakes and let that devil know that is not my thought. Satan, you are a liar and the father of lies. Hurting myself will not change anything. It would mean I took what I thought was the easy road out.

The responsibility of life was a gift given to me and I must value it. Just because someone else doesn't value me is not a reason to check out. There is still a lot of living to do. I have value and worth. I am accepted in the beloved and you are, too.

COMING HOME

There is something chasing me, following close behind that won't allow me to be me, to be free. It's not the me that you see, the well-adjusted me, knowing what I want, appearing to be free. There's an uneasy feeling, a discomfort that makes me feel that I don't fit — as if someone or something is hovering near, waiting to remind me of my past and I want to escape.

I'm home — a place that is so very familiar, yet I feel out of place, surrounded by people who say they love me and yet I feel I don't belong. I find myself looking for myself or someone to blame in this place that I call home. I want to be comfortable in my own skin in my house and embrace life but my past holds me captive, haunting me, reminding me of past failures, rejections, disappointment and let downs that plague my mind.

I project my expectations of what I think love and family should look like on the ones around me. I know something is missing. I lack relationships yet I hold everyone hostage in my mind with the hurts and disappointment I feel, allowing my feeling and thoughts to remind me of their failures but never acknowledging that I may have failed someone, too. I want to be home, present, not just existing to be a part of what's taking place around me. I want to be free in my mind, my spirit, but how do I release myself from this prison that I created in my mind?

Life seems hard, unfair, disappointing — a curse to me. My expectation seems out of reach, not realizing that I can't obtain anything without experiencing opposition. The thing is it's not there to hurt, defeat, or stop me. It's there to help me think and realize I can't do it in my strength and power. I need help. I buy into the lie of the enemy, allowing him to entertain me, while subtly reminding me of past failures, disappointment, and hurt that I experienced in this place. He helps me make excuses for my actions as if it's ok. I justify my wrong to make me feel better but my past haunts me. I must remind myself there is no victory without opposition and life will never be pain-free.

I hope I can come to a place of repentance and learn that God allows opposition that I may grow up and look to him to help in times of trouble, to learn his plan for my life, and follow him.

I must surrender my expectation for his expectation, my will for his will, or I will always find myself looking for myself, trying to find a purpose for living. There's a song that says, "The enemy can't change who I am, He can't take what I have. I belong toGod." I must know He is with me. I belong to Him and He is home with me. The only person I can change is me and that's a decision and a choice that I must make. Coming home should be a wonderful time of reconnecting with family and friends. Instead, it's overwhelming — a tremendous adjustment that requires change. The children who were little when I left have grown up and outgrown the image that lived in my mind.

That's life. We often hold images in our mind of who they were the last time I saw them, and now they are all grown up with their own ideas and dreams. I may not like their way but it's important that I learn how to reconnect and develop a relationship with them before telling them what my expectations are for them. I talk, ask questions that provoke thought, and love them where they are .... never give up on them, and I hope no one gives up on me...... while I continue to encourage and love them. I know I can only change me.

HOME FOR THANKSGIVING

Now we are in a place we long to be — home with family and learning them all over again. There have been many highs and lows, but I am grateful for them all. I wasn't grateful going through them but looking back I know God was with me as He was many years ago. Home is a place I want to be. It's in this place and time I learn to just be me. I struggled with who I am and who I'm called to be, feeling insecure about us, about your feelings for me. My expectation wasn't necessarily what I hoped it would be, but I'm reminded that everything has a season of change and nothing remains the same.

We grow older and we learn just as the children around us. They cry into this world not knowing anything except he is hungry, and he needs to be changed. So, it is with us. We are hungry for the next in our life and we need change. Many times, we are not sure how it will take place, but I know it's necessary for my life and for growth. As our children grow up, we want them to mature in every area of their life. We can't walk around living on the last meal we ate to sustain us or the last bottle to hold them for years until they can get it for themselves. Therefore, change comes to make us uncomfortable where we are and grow us up, to be sure there are a lot of hiccups along the way. I heard this saying from a pastor. She said she often told her children this, "The decisions you make in life are life changing and long lasting," so be careful how you choose and keep God first in every decision you make.

Proverbs 4: 7: Wisdom is the principal thing; therefore get wisdom and in all you getting get understanding. Proverbs 1 vs. 7: "The fear of the Lord is the beginning of knowledge, but fools despise wisdom and instruction".

Wisdom is the principal thing to get understanding. My prayer has been LORD teach me how to live this life and give we wisdom how to go in and come out to get through the struggles and the pains of life. He has been with me through it all and now we are home again. It hasn't been easy but it's doable if you keep God first.

Here we are on Thanksgiving Day, about to share in the food and love of our family — to be family connected by birth and love — a bond that's stronger than anything we know and that comes from God. I am grateful for each of you and the part that you play in my life — the things that help to shape it and grow me up, learning the things that I can endure by the grace of God. The scripture says, "It is the LORD's mercies that we are not consumed, and his compassion fail not. It's new every morning. Great is thy faithfulness."

22It is of the LORD'S mercies that we are not consumed, because his compassions fail not. 23They are new every morning: great is thy faithfulness. Lamentations 3:22-23

Life will happen to each of us, good or bad. Sometimes it will be painful but remember to put God first in all you go through. Ask him for directions and praise him because it's another day that He has kept you. I thank him for purpose and health. I thank him for good days and hard days when I make myself get up and smile and say thank you for another day. Because any day above dirt is a good day. Thanks for teaching me how to wait for You and not move out of Your timing. Sometimes we do things too quickly or slowly and we miss his plan for us.

I love this song. It says, "If I was in control of my life, I would have worked things out so much differently. There would be no hurt, no pain, no disappointment of this. My life would be scot-free but that just goes to show just how little I know about leading and controlling my life. All these things work together to make the best me" (lyrics by Shaun Pace Rhodes)

For this, I am learning to be grateful. It's all part of the plan in making me to be a better me. Home for Thanksgiving is wonderful a time and I praise God for where he has brought us from. We all have expectations, but I want His expectation to be my expectation for life with our family trusting him to be the head of our life. I didn't say it would be easy, but He will give us the strength to finish strong and leave a legacy that our children will say I serve God because he is faithful when I'm not. We have reference points that He has always been there and He reminds us how good He has been to us when we reflect on Him. Happy Thanksgiving.

> [24]**Now unto him that is able to keep you from falling, and to present you faultless before the presence of his glory with exceeding joy,** [25]**To the only wise God our Saviour, be glory and majesty, dominion and power, both now and ever. Jude 1:24-25**

MOVING FORWARD

"Only be strong and very courageous; be careful to do according to all the law which Moses My servant commanded you; do not turn from it to the right or to the left, so that you may have success wherever you go. Joshua 1:7

I keep hearing this voice in my mind that repeats all the things that I was told I'm not. I hear the lie that wants me to hide in shame, but I know a truth that keeps me moving forward. The love he gives is pure, sustaining, enduring. It's not toxic or confusing. I think it is because humans are flawed, and our proclivity to sin is a real part of us.

There is a question I often ask: How do I move forward and be what I am called to be? There's a song entitled This is Me. It talks about not being a stranger to the dark because you are broken, cast down, and feeling no one will love you the way you are. You hide your scars because of brokenness and shame. It's not of your making but what was said to you about you, your life, your birth — things you had no control over.

Today is your day. Love hung on a cross and paid a debt for you and me. His love is pure. It was poured out for humanity that is priceless. He did something for me I couldn't do for myself, and He wants a relationship with me to know me when I accept him as LORD of my life. This gives me the desire to move forward, to be strong and courageous in Him, not myself.

I've learned to surrender and just lift a finger because He is reaching down to me. The information you want is given on a need-to-know basis. Learn to follow. You are not the leader.

I am stronger because I have been empowered, I have the assurance in knowing I win. Empowerment helps me to realize there is a name of God for whatever I need and because I name the name of Christ then I should begin to look, act, and sound like my Heavenly Father.

Forward is the direction I'm going. This is Me starting new, starting over again.

I AM MY FATHER'S SON

For nine months she carried me inside, and after I was born, I was called by my father's name. You see, I'm a junior and in some ways, I look like him, too. When you're young, you want to do what your father does. I walked like him and talked like him, too because in my eyes, that's a little boy's hero. But as I grew older, my hero became tarnished and gray, not standing quite as tall and I began to wonder: how did he get this way?

This should never be. He's the one you're looking up to teach you to be a man. What happened and why is it that he seems so different now than what he used to be? When you see and hear the wrong things, it does something to that little guy down on the inside and the pain that grows starts to dim the light in a little boy's eyes. He grows up and tells himself I'll never act like him until one day the seed that was sown takes root and starts to grow.

It doesn't manifest itself all at once but little by little, it begins to show itself in little things that you will pass off as nothing, until one day you say, "Lord, how did I get here?" Show me my life because now you're a father, with a son looking at you. You did all the things you said you would not do even when you said you didn't want to act like that.

I will show more love, and my children will know that I am there. I'll make sure they know their value and worth. I find that I am indeed my father's son, not because I wear his name but I did some of the same things he did. I may not have done everything he did but that's not the point. The fact that I did it was too much. I began to ponder and pray, and asked the Lord how many males have had this seed passed along to them.

I thought about my son, nephews, cousin, and uncles — my kin. What kind of legacy was left for us and what kind are we leaving behind? My daughters and sisters and nieces that will one day be wives will want real men, Godly men to lead and walk beside. I began to weep for me, for us, for them — the ones that came before me and the ones that will come after we are gone. I cried for homes that have been broken and the hearts and spirits that need to be mended. I cried out to the Lord because I did it wrong and I want to get it right. I want to be a Godly man — a man with a standard and know his value and his worth. Lord, I want to have integrity to be faithful to God, my wife, my family, my house. Lord, I don't want to be that man anymore; heal and deliver me. I want to overcome this so that my sons and grandsons will not have to struggle with that. Take control of my life. Fill and heal me of my past that I may embrace my future and heal the little boy inside of every man.

"Lord, help me to stand and as I pray for every man that has ever struggled with this, guide me dear Lord, with your mercy and grace, and thank you for today. I am an overcomer because You found me and filled me with your love, so now I know that I am My Father's son.

MY MOUTH

There is something in me that I find difficult to tame: I would like to control what I say. The word speaks of it, and it should not be, but anger comes quickly, and I don't stop or control what I say I just release a fury of words spoken in haste. The scripture says:

There is one who speaks rashly like the thrusts of a sword {Proverbs 12:18} and my tongue was not wise it didn't bring healing.

James 3:8 say but the tongue can no man tame; {it is} an unruly evil, full of deadly poison; another scripture says a soft answer turneth away wrath: but grievous words stir up anger {Proverbsf 15:1}.

I know these things and I still struggle with them. Why does this plague me so? I don't like me after I speak words that hurt and wound because I didn't take time to think before I spoke. It did not give God glory although I had prayed and blessed someone that was not in my house. I want my mouth and tongue to be wholesome and a tree of life. I don't want a breach in my spirit because of perverseness {Proverbs 15:4}. The word says that my tongue is like the pen of a ready writer {psalm 45:1} and another scripture in Proverb 13:3 says He that keepeth his mouth keepeth his life: but he that openeth wide his lips shall have destruction. A fool uttereth all his mind: but a wise man keepeth it in till afterward {Proverb 29:11}.

My mouth is unruly and it speaks out of turn. Now is the time for me to make a change, to stop making excuses step out and take a chance. I asked Him, and He extended His hand to me and there is no sense in me acting like I don't know what it takes. We all have something we struggle with in life and please know that is not an excuse. Your struggle may not be mine but we all struggle in or with something in this life.

It's time to stop confusing the issue and acting or pretending like I'm convincing the people and myself that it's said in love and tempered with grace when I know fully well it was all the things it should not be. The things that the scriptures speak for us not to do — we should be drawing them with love and kindness — seasoning our speech with salt and allowing it to be tempered with mercy and grace.

We know that God has done all he is going to do and some things are left up to us. He gave his Son and his Son gave his life. Did we really think we could just sit down and do nothing while letting him take care of everything that happens in our lives? There are some things we must want to change in ourselves. He gave us His Word and we must allow the Word to work in us. You see it in others and you want it for yourself but you're not willing to put in the work. We talk about change but we don't really believe it can happen to us.

You say I'll take small steps. He did it for them so I know He will do it for me. Then you wait but you don't practice what you read. He gave us a promise, principles, provision, and a problem and the answer is found in His Word.

Now as I sit here pondering all of this, I know for sure I won't put it off for tomorrow for tomorrow may be too late. So I'll start it today. I may slip and fall sometime but the good thing about it is I don't have to stay down and neither do you. So if you're having a struggle in what you say just read the word and let it work for you. Blessing and cursing should not come from the same fountain so speak blessing as we grow together, allowing the Word to work in our mouth.

LIFE'S LESSON FROM MAMA

*In life, if everything is given to you, you will not learn anything. If you don›t see or learn from the situations that happen*ed before, you would take it for granted that it will always be this way. If you never had to struggle or go through anything, you couldn't or wouldn't survive when the chips are down Life teaches us lessons if we are willing to pay attention and listen. Now let's consider the butterfly. It doesn't have a mother to watch over it. The caterpillar gives up its life for the butterfly to have life. The butterfly must struggle coming out of the chrysalis, or it will not survive. If the wings are not strong, if they are deformed because it didn't go through something, it will die because there is no strength to do the things it needs to for survival. Look at the giraffe. The baby has to fall at least 6 feet to the ground on its back and then stand on its wobbly legs. He may get knocked down again and he has to get back up. To us, this seems cruel but in the wild, if he doesn't stand on his feet he will die because predators are waiting for a good meal. Elephants born in the wild must stand on their 4 legs after birth, and their mother may kick them down or knock it around after birth. He must get back up each time. It is a hard task, but this is a lesson for his survival life in the wild.

They must understand survival is important even when the herd is there to protect them. The question in my mind is, "Why is this so hard for most humans?" We allow children a free pass in survival skills. They are babied and carried and can't do anything for themselves — tie their shoes, follow instructions, clean up after themselves, and respect their elders and friends. These animals love their young, but they must learn the lesson being taught to them because it is a necessary skill in life to make it and survive another day. We are to train up a child in the way he should go and when he is old he will not depart from it. What happened?

LIFE'S RHYTHM

Your life has a rhythm, a swing, a beat of poetic motion, a song that stirs your heart and set your feet in motion. Joy and sunshine describe your smile, and your laughter is like the waters of a sparkling brook. You're caring, compassionate and kind and a wonderful gift to all that know you. You're a treasure that has not yet been found.

You are a strong woman with character, passionate and true, often misunderstood because you are so direct. Many times, you are thought to be too outspoken. In many cases it is a quality that serves you well because there is no mistake about where you are coming from.

You are precious and beloved by those who know you well. You are a rare diamond that sways and dances to the beat of your drum. There are not many with that style. You bounce back in the face of adversity because what you go through is not who you are, nor does it define you. It's a stepping stone for where you are going.

Your life is not defined by circumstances because when you can love regardless of the situation that is a true test of character and strength. You learn not to blame but face the truth and with truth you can overcome anything.

You are faithful and forgiving, and you know how to extend grace. You see, we are all in need of grace not because we deserve it but it was extended to us when the Son went to the cross. You are kind and stern but gentle, a friend for real. You're transparent — the real deal —although you will speak what's on your mind.

Always remember who you are. A woman can be right and still be wrong. You don't have to prove anything. Just stand strong, speaking the truth. Mama always said that when you do that you only have to do it once.

You don't have to stoop to another person's level or allow someone to cause you to be less than who you are to make a point; LaShunda, just be you because that's what you do. You are not defined by the color of your skin, the texture of your hair, or what you wear because baby, you can make a sack look good. You got it like that.

A man at your side doesn't say who you are. You are the treasure that he seeks and the incubator that holds a man's dreams.

You don't have to look for him because he that findeth a wife finds a good thing and obtains favor from the LORD. Remember that you are his favor and it's not because you are lost but quality just doesn't come cheap, and he must know what he is getting to call you his own. Stand up, baby, and take a bow. It's your life's rhythm in motion.

> *21Life and death are in the power of the tongue, and those who love it will eat its fruit. 22He who finds a wife finds a good thing and obtains favor from the LORD.*
>
> *23The poor man pleads for mercy, but the rich man answers harshly.*
>
> *24A man of many companions may come to ruin, but there is a friend who stays closer than a brother. Proverbs 18: 21-24*

BEING MY OWN KIND OF BEAUTIFUL

Being my own kind of beautiful is just me being me,
not what everyone says I am,
but I want to be the kind of person God designed me to be.
There is a quote from Shakespeare that says:
To thine own self be true. To be true to myself
I must know who I am, and what is expected of me,
from my parents and those that are over me.
It's not about what society or TV and magazine pictures
say beauty is because that's a changing
fad; nor what my peers may say beautiful is....
they are still learning and growing just like me.
They say when you laugh the world laughs with you,
but sometimes they will laugh at you so be
the first to laugh at yourself.
You see what works for you may not necessarily work for me.
We are uniquely different in our own special way
so I must be my own kind of beautiful in my
most unique way.
I am respectful, I am courteous, and confident,
I am helpful, kind, and considerate.
It's important to be considerate of others;
I treat people the way I want to be treated.
I am honest with myself, and I try to be honest with others,
you see it's not about being right all

the time because you can be right and still be wrong.
I am trustworthy, I am learning my self-worth
because I am valuable to me and my parents. I
am learning to be happy just being me.
I have potential and I am learning every day the type of
young lady I want to be. I have value,
courage to stand for what is right and to know that my
self-worth is not for sale.

7-2-15 tsj
Updated 2/18/2017

A BETTER ME

There is a person I want to be. The person I aspire to be is not just the me you see, but a better me. I want to be better than I am right now. I don't ever want to feel that I have arrived. There's more to life and so much I have not yet realized. A better me will allow me to understand that there are different degrees of greatness and compassion. It's not measured by what I think I know. To be a better me is to be better today than I was yesterday and apply the principles and values that are being taught by parents, pastors, and teachers and all that have rule over me and the word of God.

I must ask myself who I helped up.speak life to what I do with the gifts and talents God gave me. Pastor always says, "the decisions you make are life changing and long lasting," so the decision I make to be a better me causes me to search deep within. I will ask the hard questions. Did I do my best? Did I pray about it? or did I decide what was best for me? Did I inspire or encourage someone to be great in what they are called to do?

Do better next time. Don't settle for the last great move. There is more –there are different degrees of great and good. There are second chances. Go farther, dream bigger. As I was encouraged and motivated, I want to encourage someone else and help him to encourage and motive others.

To be a better me I must have my own I-am statement, and I must learn to affirm myself, to tell myself that I am enough, and that my broke days are over lack and slack has no place in my life. I am fearfully and wonderfully made and my soul knoweth right well. I have God ideas that are bigger than me. I won't stop because of fear. It is part of the process, and I am not afraid because I know He's preparing me for greatness. I'm tailor-made for this.

To be a better me, I must remember where I came from and how I got to where I am. Knowing that I stand on the shoulders of prayer warriors and intercessors who have prayed me through things before it happened. They decreed and declared a thing and called my angels to watch over me. They annulated illicit lifestyles and generational curses that may have been in my blood line, but they won't come near me or my children and grandchildren.

When I fall, I don't have to stay down. I can get back up and get in line again because it's a choice and a decision that I make. The fall wasn't permanent but a lesson to be learned. To be a better me, I must PUSH (Pray Until Something Happens) and not stop. It's not just for me but for the ones who are watching me, following me, and coming after me.

To be a better me I must learn that living life my way is not "the way" and the examples that I learn, and follow are the ones that have been taught to me in the word of God.

Pastor ministered a word about the olive, letting us know that we too will go through so God can get the best from us. It won't destroy you but it will grow you up, strengthen you, and help you to be a better you, so I must pay attention. The olive must be crushed and pressed. The process is not gentle. So it is with life. The press won't break me. It's to make me. The process is producing something in me and in life there are different stages to the process. I learned that God allows us to go through in life but it for my good. I may not understand it while it's happening to me and in me, but it will yield a peaceable fruit. To be a better me, I too must learn to yield to the process that God is teaching me. To be a better me, I must know who I am and whose I am. I must know that I am a vessel full of power and it must be in me, not on me.

[8)]But I am like a green olive tree in the house of God: I trust in the mercy of God forever and ever. [9)]I will praise thee forever, because thou hast don it. I will wait on thy name; for it is good before thy saints: Psalms 52:8-9

REAL GIRLS ROCK

For every real girl who grows up and becomes a young lady, this is to let you know that real girls do rock. You may wonder how we rock. Just sit a spell and listen to this tale.

You are fearfully and wonderfully made, and your soul knows it right well and it is not by chance or happenstance. I am not defined by what has happened to me. Life will happen whether young or old and you don't have control over that. Therefore, it will not define me or what I will be. I am beautiful inside and out and it's not about my complexion or skin tone. Real beauty begins on the inside of you, and I rise despite adversity because my destiny waits.

It's not who my parents are or where I am from. It is because I'm a real girl and I am here to stay. I'm encouraged to study to learn and grow and I refuse to let life circumstances get me down. I'm poised and there's something on the inside that tells me I was born for greatness. If you are just looking at me trying to judge by what you see, you may miss it because you don't know my value, and you can't ascertain my worth.

You may think I am just fooling myself, but you don't know I have real pedigree. I am the real deal, true grit, the lasting kind I don't have to carouse or show off just to be seen. It's not my style. You see, I'm not about that flash, flaunting, or bling. You may think I'm bragging, and I might, but it's not in a boastful way. It's the truth — what my Heavenly Father told me I am.

He said I am the head and not the tail. I'm above only and I'm not beneath. I'm rich and I'm not poor. I am a lender and never a borrower, and I can do all things through Him who strengthens me. This tells me I don't have to think little or belittle in my own eyes or anyone else's because I'm important to Him. Besides, I'm a real girl and I rock.

HEARING THE HEART OF LOVE OUR WEDDING DAY

I watch him stand at the altar, knowing he is waiting for his bride. Many emotions flood my mind knowing what it took for us to get to this place in time. Walking towards my future, my husband, waiting for me, our lives will change, for the good and the betterment of us and our family. I am bone of his bone and flesh of his flesh and today we will become one.

Life does not always look the way we think it should and surely it is never quite the way we picture it in our dreams. But it is real, and God's loving plan brought us here. The Word tells us that He knows the plan that He has for us plan of good and not evil and to give us an expected end. Although we have plans often, it doesn't line up with God's plan, but we know His plan will be completed in us. I know this is real and not a dream. I'm living it as I walk with my father. He will once again give me to my soul mate.

I see the man I love with every fiber of my being and know that he feels the same way about me. I know he was willing to fight for me, for our relationship, our life. I know him and he knows me and understands the magnitude of this relationship and the love we share. My heart is full to overflowing and I am not sure if I can contain all that I feel right now.

As I walk into my future with my husband, I remember we had life issues that we had to get right to move forward and it is not a surprise to either of us because we are broken people. It took faith in God and each other to get to this place. It was not a question of separation but we be honest with ourselves, while standing here looking in the face of ugly and adversity and all we think we know. *Lets pause right here and let that sink in for a moment.* The question is: Can we love each other for real, despite our differences and get to a place of forgiveness acceptance and agreement? You see, there is a place you got to go just to get there and there are some things we must leave behind just to get there. But when we get there, there is a new beginning.

As the magnitude of all of this unfolds before me, my mind is in a whirlwind to grasp the emotions I am experiencing. I knew the process and the fight to endure getting to this place was God.

I was dressed in a beautiful gown with hair and makeup done to perfection. No one except God, the preacher, and we knew what we had endured. We stood before our families, the people, and our pastor to recite our vows of truth and love. Everything in me cried for the love I have for this man and the future we would share, leaving a legacy for our children and family.

It took ten years of dying to self, ten years of holding on to faith in God, ten years of letting go, learning to understand each other and knowing that both of us had to come to a place of agreement. To really understand the power of agreement for us, It took ten years to release all the pent-up frustration, misunderstanding that we walked around with, keeping our feelings and emotions in check, but not in check.— discovering us and loving each other despite our brokenness and understanding that we have fault.; We know we are not willing to give up on each other.

You discover that love is a bond that is stronger than any mistake that happens in life when you can love for real. When you can love for real knowing yes, I missed it. We missed it. Yes, we were wrong about that. My emotions got in the way; I was judging instead of hearing your heart. Yes, I can forgive and not hold it against you because we must understand we are broken people in need of a healer.

We came together understanding we came from different backgrounds, with different life experiences — humans with faults and failures, different but the same. We came together loving and forgiving each other without keeping tallies or scores of who did what to whom, but learning to build each other up, learning that when you are successful, I am successful. We are one. We are learning to be accountable to each other in our action and the decisions we make. We make each other look good and we are better together. We are learning how to love in the good and bad when life happens. We are treating each other with respect without derogatory verbiage.

This is our promise to each other: we will not leave one another behind because we want to reflect our commitment to God in our life and our love for one another and to our children. We are in this love together and we are in it to win together as a whole family unit.

Mr Travis & Mrs. Alexandria Andrews

AN ENCOUNTER WITH LOVE

As I pen these words it is truly from my heart. Getting you to know you has been a pleasure. When I saw you from afar, I knew you would be my life partner. As I watched you, your beauty left me speechless I felt destiny had placed us in the right place at the right time. Working with my family has afforded me an opportunity that I can only thank God for his grace and mercy towards me because today I have encountered love.

I didn't know how this would play out, but I knew what I wanted, and I know that God has a plan for us. So, I give him thanks and praise in advance for placing you in my life and afford us the opportunity to get to know each other. This has been an awesome experience and I wouldn't change it for anything because it teaches us something if we pay attention. In life we will have bumps in the road. They are called disagreements, but it helps us to grow together, learning each other's rhythm. Learning how to dance together and allowing me to lead is a receipt for a great relationship. With this comes understanding, love, and patience and making sure to keep God first makes for a great journey into life together.

I want you to hear my heart and take a journey through life with me. I will do everything in my power to build you up as a woman, and I pray you will do the same for me as a man. I don't want to take anything for granted. We will make mistakes, but the mistakes are not there to hurt us but for us to learn from them together.

I want to be the best man that I can be to love you and treat you as my queen. I may not be able to give you a lot of material things, but I can make sure I give you the best of me as we make lasting memories as we grow together on this journey through life. I know that disagreement happens in relationships, and you will be angry with me for one reason or another, but I won't run from you. I won't leave you to wonder. I will stand by your side, willing to learn until we get it right. Life is not always fair or fun, but it can be an amazing experience and I want to enjoy it with you as we grow together. When the road dips and one of us stumble, I want us to prop each other up.

I want you as my life partner. It takes love, prayer, and faith in each other to sustain a relationship as we look to God to guide us. When hard times come along, and life happens to us and around us and there are days we agree to disagree, I still want to do life with you. Love is not the absence of pain. They exist on the same plan. We must learn how to love and embrace life as it happens, but it is through growth and maturing in our thinking and communication that we get better and become stronger together, and every day, I want to do life with you. To share and experience life together we will cry together and laugh together, hold hands and watch a sunset or take a drive and share an ice cream cup. It's learning to laugh at yourself and to say, "Me too," even when there are tears. I want you to feel safe and protected, never abandoned or left behind.

I never want you to feel that you must be less than who you are to make me feel good about myself. Confidence is knowing who you are becoming and being willing to strive to be better every day. We are continually changing, and I want to celebrate life and its changes with you. That means all the accomplishments and near misses. We don't have defeats; we have do overs. If God allows us to see another day, this is another opportunity to try again and think outside of the box, We will just ask Him to show us the way.

I don't want to wear a mask with you. I want to be free, and I want you to be free to be the best you and me we can be. To encounter love on this day has been such a blessing. I am looking forward to doing life with you.

All My Love

ABOUT THE BOOK

I started this little project because I felt this pull or call to keep writing. It wasn't easy to be transparent, to bare your soul for everyone to read. But by the grace of God I made it through this. Behind the Mask came to me one day when I was look at a program that a pastor I know was going to be speaking. The mask spoke to me. We have become accustomed to hiding in shame.

Hiding becomes a way of life for many. It can be mental, physical, and emotional. Sometimes it comes to a point where you can't hide anymore. I pray this book is encouraging and you can see you through these pages of this book — what you aspire and what you want to change.

ABOUT THE AUTHOR

TAMIE SAVAGE JOHNSON, the author of *Over Whelming Victories in all these Difficulties*, wrote her first book while living in North Carolina. She now lives in Florida with her husband surrounded by family. Tamie is a speaker and encourager. She enjoys serving in her home church and assisting her son in his Ministry.

*My desire is to live a life that is poured out and
to be all that God is calling me to be.*

PART ONE

I had to go through it to be productive and whole because who I was is not who I am and there is still hope. I know there is purpose in waiting even in the times we live in. We struggle behind the mask but we must learn to be grateful for the struggle and know we are broken to be free.... so we can move to the next.

PART TWO

We are human buildings under construction. We are constantly changing, and we live behind a mask. I often wonder when we will ever grow up. Unfortunately, some of us never do, but I know that I am next. How I stand in these shoes is a question, but I have a choice for life. Sometimes you are in the room again trying to rebuild the wall of family and relationships. Follow me to a place of compassion and encouragement to heal a heart.

PART THREE

He called you beautiful but sometimes you don't know that he is talking to you. He wants you to know that you are tailor-made and you have to live it, saved and sassy even when you turn sixty. There are days that I am looking at myself and strength and honor are my clothing. Ring the bell of faith and accomplishment to crossing over. #forgiveme #forgiveyou #forgivethem is forgiving everyone to perspective in anger and there are times you don't know that you have to let go. Coming home is wonderful when you can move forward. It's important to know who you are and watch your mouth. There are lessons to learn from mama and life has a rhythm, so be your own kind of beautiful. Real girls rock. One day there will be an encounter with love. Listen to the heart of love on your wedding day.

CPSIA information can be obtained
at www.ICGtesting.com
Printed in the USA
BVHW041450240223
659176BV00003B/388